Village Walks
in
NOTTINGHAMSHIRE

Village Walks
in
NOTTINGHAMSHIRE

Peter Fooks

COUNTRYSIDE BOOKS
NEWBURY BERKSHIRE

COUNTRYSIDE BOOKS
3 Catherine Road
Newbury Berkshire

ISBN 1 85306 503 X

Designed by Graham Whiteman
Maps and photographs by the author
Illustrations by Trevor Yorke
Front cover photo of Kersall taken by Bill Meadows

Produced through MRM Associates Ltd., Reading
Typeset by Techniset Typesetters, Newton-le-Willows
Printed by Woolnough Bookbinding Ltd., Irthlingborough

Contents

AREA MAP SHOWING LOCATIONS OF THE WALKS

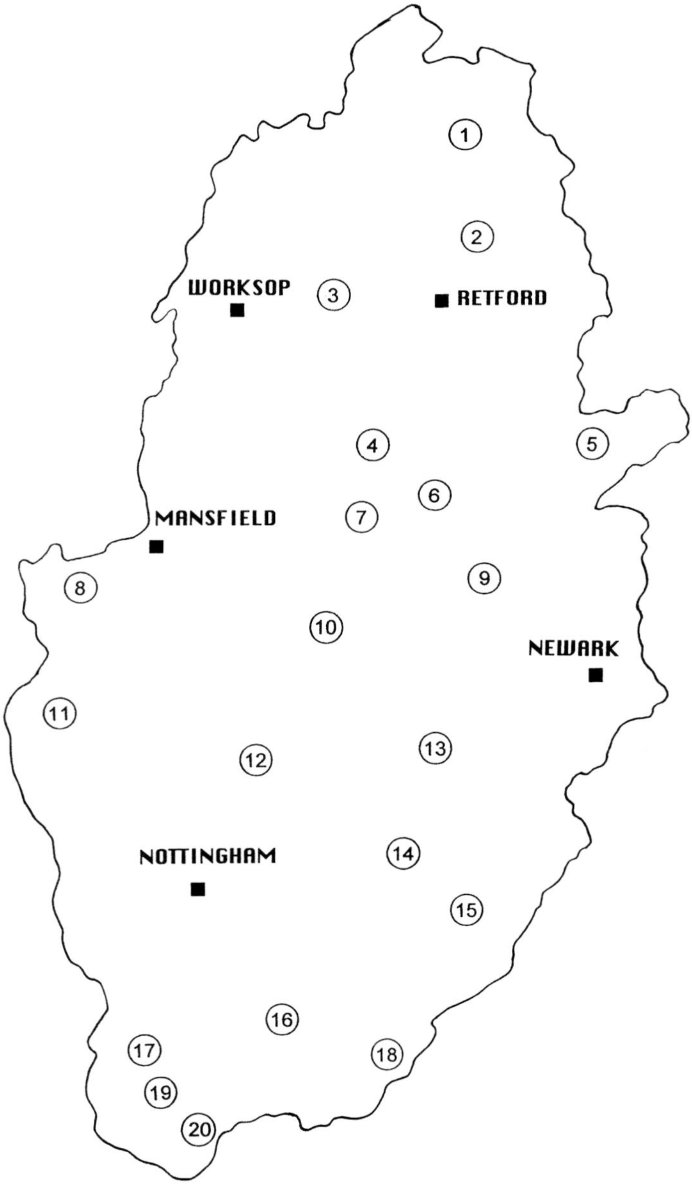

① 1

② 2

WORKSOP
■ ③ 3   ■ **RETFORD**

④ 4   ⑤ 5

⑥ 6

MANSFIELD   ⑦ 7
■

⑨ 9

⑧ 8

⑩ 10

NEWARK
■

⑪ 11

⑫ 12   ⑬ 13

⑭ 14

NOTTINGHAM
■

⑮ 15

⑯ 16

⑰ 17   ⑱ 18

⑲ 19

⑳ 20

WALK

Acknowledgement

The assistance, in particular, of the Rights of Way Department of the Nottinghamshire County Council in verifying the existence of rights of way is gratefully acknowledged.

Publisher's Note

We hope that you obtain considerable enjoyment from this book; great care has been taken in its preparation. Although at the time of publication all routes followed public rights of way or permitted paths, diversion orders can be made and permissions withdrawn.

We cannot of course be held responsible for such diversion orders and any inaccuracies in the text which result from these or any other changes to the routes, nor any damage which might result from walkers trespassing on private property. We are anxious though that all details covering the walks are kept up to date and would therefore welcome information from readers which would be relevant to future editions.

Introduction

The English village has seen many changes down the years, and nowhere more so than here in Nottinghamshire. The village of Hickling, for instance, once had its own dressmaker, tailor, saddler, grocer, butcher, wheelwright, miller and punt-maker. It now has none of these, and most local people commute to Nottingham or Melton for their work.

The changing needs of industry have also made their mark. As the demand for coal expanded, so new pits were opened, and villages whose economy depended mainly on agriculture became, in effect, two villages, with a new, largely independent mining estate springing up alongside the older agricultural community. Now the wheel has turned full circle. The pits are shut down and, here again, the displaced workers have had to learn new skills — and commute.

Expanding population has had its effects, and villages which, within living memory, were still small, unspoilt, self-sufficient communities have grown into small towns or, in many cases, have been absorbed into the larger conurbations.

Despite all this, most of our villages retain a vibrant, independent spirit, with the new 'in-comers' making a full contribution to the local scene; be it church, pub, parish council or whatever. And the traditional village atmosphere survives and flourishes.

Our Nottinghamshire countryside still retains a network of quiet lanes, footpaths and bridleways, linking the towns and villages of the county, and providing access to a wealth of attractive and historical scenery and sites. There have been changes, of course, and some paths have been diverted, or lost completely. But others have been added to the network — significantly, as at Teversal, with the conversion to recreational use of a number of obsolete mineral railway lines.

This book will, we hope, introduce the reader to a few of our most interesting and historical villages, and to some of the delightful paths, lanes and byways that surround them. The standard of walking is generally easy, with circular routes of varying length — from $3^1/_2$ mile strolls to a couple of slightly more energetic, but infinitely rewarding, 7 mile rambles. And the terrain includes woods and pastures, rivers and canals (the county of Nottinghamshire has an abundance of waterways), as well as old railways, prehistoric sites and historic buildings.

The sketch maps included here are for general guidance only, and should not be regarded as definitive. I have included details of the relevant Ordnance Survey sheets required in each case, and use of these is strongly recommended. Many people make do with the Landranger ($1^1/_4$ inch to a mile) series, although I prefer the Pathfinder — or the new Explorer where this is available — which, at $2^1/_2$ inches to the mile, carries greater detail.

Each of the walks starts and finishes at a featured village, and basic details for reaching that village are provided including, for those without personal transport, information on available bus or rail services.

For those coming by car, parking will be a necessary consideration. Not many villages have a public car park although, in most cases, you will find it possible to park alongside one or other of the village streets. But always do so with full regard for other users — especially, of course, the residents of the village. If you are using the village pub, the landlord may well permit you to leave your car in his car park for the duration of your walk. But do not take his permission for granted. Ask.

Which brings me to food and drink. All of the villages featured here have some form of catering facility — even if it is only a post office with crisps and lemonade! This is not intended as a book of 'pub walks' but, in the nature of things, most of the caterers identified are, in fact, pubs. A few Nottinghamshire villages have cafes — but not many — and some of them no longer possess a post office. But today's village pub is much more of a family venue than it used to be. All of those identified provide bar food — snacks as well as full meals, and it is not necessary to buy alcohol. I myself am a lifelong 'single half' man, while my wife, who has accompanied me on most of these walks, never drinks anything stronger than coffee. What we cannot guarantee, of course, is that any of the caterers will be open when you arrive — so it is a wise precaution to carry a snack with you, against drought, famine, or early closing. Telephone numbers have been given wherever possible so that you can, if you wish, check opening hours in advance of your visit.

Clothing and equipment should be no great problem. You should, of course, have suitable footwear — and be prepared to pick up a little mud here and there. And you should adapt your clothing to suit the existing and likely climatic conditions. It is as well to carry light waterproofs in case the weather turns sour on you. And a simple first aid kit; and those emergency rations. And it is easier if you have a light day-sack to carry them in. If you also want to take a camera, or binoculars, fair enough. And don't forget your map. And this book!

And now I think I've said quite enough. Enjoy your walking!

Peter Fooks

GRINGLEY ON THE HILL

Length: 5½ miles

Getting there: Gringley on the Hill lies on the north side of the A631 (Bawtry-Gainsborough) road, about 3 miles west of Beckingham.

Public transport: Roadcar services 96/97 Retford-Gainsborough, hourly,

Monday to Saturday, with four Sunday journeys; 83 Worksop-Gainsborough, Monday to Saturday, two to three journeys; 98/98x Lincoln-Doncaster (jointly with Eagre Coaches), Monday to Saturday, six journeys.

Parking: Alongside Gringley High Street.

Maps: OS Landranger 112 Scunthorpe; Pathfinder 728 Harworth and Gringley (GR 736907).

At first sight, the reference to a hill in the village's name might be considered a little presumptuous. But it must be remembered that the land to the north – from which direction the eminence is best observed – is fenland, grading down, in a matter of a couple of miles, to as near sea-level as makes no odds.

Gringley is a conservation area, so there is very little intrusion from modern devel-

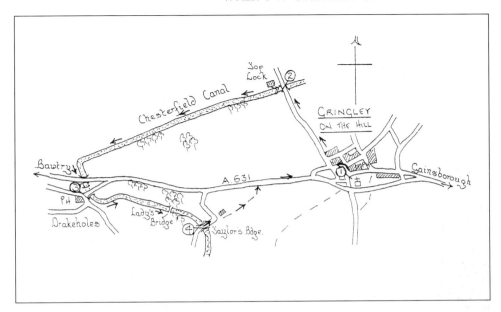

opment. A particular blessing has been the construction of a bypass, which takes through traffic away from the village and which has, undoubtedly, saved the butter cross from total destruction!

The village appears to enjoy a long-standing tradition of nonconformity. One of the bells in the church's ancient bell-tower dates back to the Commonwealth period, when such frivolities as bells were frowned upon. And it is said that, during the same period, illegal Christmas Communion services were still conducted. In more recent times, one former vicar refused to transfer his allegiance to the newly created Diocese of Southwell and insisted on maintaining his loyalty to Lincoln. He made his point abundantly clear to visiting officials over the barrel of a shotgun. When this incumbent died in 1910 the church was falling into ruin, and his successor is to be commended for his success in restoring the building.

The walk follows a section of one of Nottinghamshire's longest canals – the Chesterfield, which crosses the county, west to east, from Shireoaks to West Stockwith. No commercial traffic uses the canal today, although the waterway is still navigable and, if you are lucky, you may catch the occasional narrow boat negotiating the lock by Gringley Bridge. You will certainly see plenty of wildfowl, as well as a few anglers and fellow walkers.

THE WALK

❶ Leave High Street via Cross Hill (by the butter cross), travelling north. Turn left at West Wells Lane and then right at the next crossroads, into Wood Lane. Follow the road down the hill to Gringley Bridge and the Chesterfield Canal.

❷ Join the towpath, following the canal

Drakeholes, a basin on the Chesterfield Canal.

FOOD and DRINK

Gringley's local is the Blue Bell, on Main Street, though from Monday to Friday, this is an 'evening only' house. Telephone: 01777 817406. The village post office is also on Main Street, as is a separate village store (associated with the local garage) and some snack materials can be obtained from either of these outlets. On the route of the walk there is the Griff Inn, an impressive building overlooking a basin on the Chesterfield Canal at Drakeholes. This provides bar food at lunchtime and in the evening, seven days a week, for example, open sandwiches, 'lite bites', ploughman's lunches and salads. The Griff also serves a varied à la carte menu, as well as full Sunday lunches. Telephone: 01777 817206.

---

west and passing Gringley Top Lock. Peaceful walking now follows, along a well-tended green track. When we last came, no boats were in evidence, but there were plenty of wildfowl and not a few anglers, as well as a walker or two, to add interest to the walk. After $1^1/_2$ miles the canal bends left, passing beneath the main road, and enters a short length of tunnel. Follow the track up to the road and turn right for Drakeholes, and the Griff Inn.

❸   Rejoin the canal at the basin, opposite the Griff, and continue, passing beneath Lady's Bridge and through Wiseton Gardens, still following the towpath.

❹ At Taylor's Bridge, ascend to the road, then cross the bridge and continue to the next bend, by the entrance to Wiseton Lodge. A notice here suggests that the drive is private, but a pedestrian right of way gives access, as far as the turning to the Lodge.

Where the drive bends left, continue ahead beside the hedge*. Part-way over the field (the path is only lightly used and the precise point may not be obvious), cross through to the opposite side of the hedge and continue over a second field. In the third field, turn left and follow the hedge to a stile and the main (A631) road. Turn right for Gringley.

*Note: The footpath from Wiseton Lodge may be difficult to follow if there is a growing crop in the fields. It is worth mentioning that, for the extra distance involved, the road offers a sensible option in case of doubt.

PLACES of INTEREST

Mattersey Priory ruins (GR 703896) stand a mile to the east of the village of Mattersey, on the banks of the river Idle, at the end of a rough track. The remains of a Gilbertine priory (founded by St Gilbert of Sempringham) this was the only house in the county belonging to the order. The ruins are in the care of English Heritage, and are open daily. The **Miniature World Museum**, Beechfield House, Main Street in West Stockwith, north-east of Gringley, is open Wednesday to Sunday and bank holidays (not January). The museum houses Nita Hardy's collection of over 600 dolls and 40 dolls' houses, as well as detailed shops and street scenes created by the proprietor herself. Telephone: 01427 890982.

CLARBOROUGH

Length: 6 miles

<table>
<tr><td>Getting there: Clarborough is on the A620 (Retford-Gainsborough) road, about 2½ miles from Retford.

Public transport: Routes 95, 96 and 97 (Roadcar)</td><td>Retford-Gainsborough, hourly service Monday to Saturday, four to eight Sunday journeys.

Parking: Roadside only; preferably (with care) on one</td><td>of the side roads.

Maps: OS Landranger 120 Mansfield and Worksop; Pathfinder 745 East Retford and Blyth (GR 731835).</td></tr>
</table>

Clarborough has grown a lot since the last war, having been designated a growth area by the County Council. As a result, the population has increased by about two-thirds to its present level of around 1,600. Despite this expansion, and its situation along the main Gainsborough road, it is still charming and unspoilt. The Chesterfield Canal passes close by the village and, along with the range of hills to the east, provides recreational opportunities for resident and visitor alike. Lying as it does so close to Retford, and with good communications, Clarborough today is some-

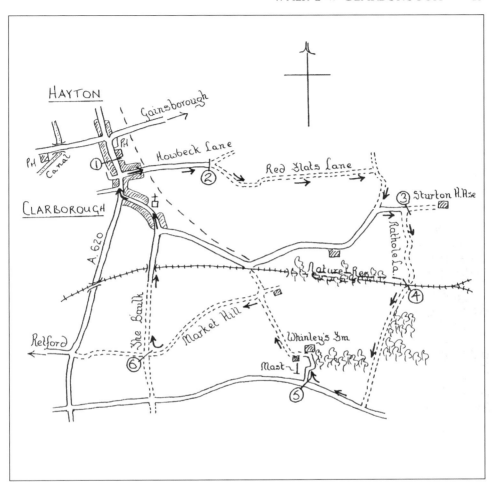

thing of a dormitory village, but it is pleasing to note that there is a full range of activities available here for all age groups.

This walk leaves the canal towpath for another day and takes to the hills, enjoying wide views in every direction. Part-way round, there is also the opportunity to visit the Clarborough Tunnel Nature Reserve. Most of the walking is along pleasant green lanes. It has not escaped the writer's

attention that the fieldpaths in this area are largely un-walked. This could have something to do with the fact that there are so many delightful green lanes hereabouts, offering a more than adequate alternative!

THE WALK
❶ Leave Clarborough via Howbeck Lane, climbing the hill away from the village.

The railway crossing at Rathole Lane.

❷   Where the road branches, take the turning on the right (Red Flats Lane). The

FOOD and DRINK

The King's Arms on Main Street is a pleasant and unspoilt traditional village inn and provides a genuine welcome. Food is served daily from 12 noon until 2 pm. A wide range of daily specials is displayed on the bar-room blackboard. Telephone: 01777 701246. The well-stocked village post office and general store, also on Main Street, offers a variety of snack items, including freshly-made sandwiches. A little off the route of the walk, beside the canal on Smeath Lane, the Gate Inn also provides bar snacks. Telephone: 01777 703397.

road soon reverts to a green lane, providing easy, peaceful walking, with only the song of a skylark to disturb the quietude. There are distant views from here – it is said that, on a clear day, you can see Lincoln Cathedral, as well as parts of Derbyshire and South Yorkshire. A dominant feature at any time, closer to hand, is the West Burton Power Station!

At the end of Red Flats Lane, turn right into Blue Stocking Lane – another green lane – and follow it to a metalled road. Turn left and continue, towards Sturton High House. From this point, two power stations are visible (though not too intrusive); West Burton and Cottam, respectively to the left and right of the farm.

❸ Turn right before the farm, descending the quaintly named Rathole Lane, to arrive at a gated railway crossing. A stile on the right here gives access to the Rathole Lane Nature Reserve, which occupies a 13 acre site alongside the railway cutting and over the Clarborough Tunnel. A woodland meander round the reserve is well worth while, and will add about 1¹/₂ miles to your total journey. (It is not possible to use the reserve as a short cut back to Clarborough, as any exits other than Rathole Lane involve trespass.)

❹ The railway line is still in use, although the crossing is unmanned; so stop, look and listen before crossing – with care. Follow the track to the road and turn right, continuing up the hill to a turning on the right, close to a tall radio mast.

❺ Turn right, passing the mast and continuing round the double bend to Whinleys Farm. Go left here, and then right, opposite another farm building, into Whinleys Lane. Initially a wooded footpath, the track develops into a green lane. At a four-way junction, turn left into Market Hill (yet another green lane) and continue to the next crossways.

❻ Turn right, and follow The Baulk and then Church Lane back to Clarborough.

PLACES of INTEREST

North Leverton Windmill, Mill Lane, North Leverton. A working windmill, fully restored and open to visitors. Contact K. Barlow, West View, Sturton Road, North Leverton, DN22 0AB. Telephone: 01427 880573 (Home) or 01427 880662 (Mill). **Sundown Adventureland** in Treswell Road, Rampton, to the south-east of Clarborough, is specially designed with young children in mind, with a wide variety of attractions, including a smugglers' cove, Shot Gun City, Rocky Mountain railroad and so on. Open daily from 10 am until 6 pm (4 pm in winter). Closed 25/26 December. Telephone: 01777 248274.

RANBY

Length: 5 miles

Getting there: Ranby is situated alongside (east of) the main A1 trunk road at its junction with the A620 (Retford) and the B6079 (Worksop) roads.

Public transport: Stagecoach East Midlands daily services 42 Retford-Worksop and 136 Retford-Tuxford-Nottingham serve Ranby.

Parking: On-street parking is possible anywhere along the main village street (Blyth Road), but the best place, bearing in mind the convenience of the residents, is where the old road runs alongside the A1.

Maps: OS Landranger 120 Mansfield and Worksop; Pathfinder 745 East Retford and Blyth (GR 650812).

There was a time when the little village of Ranby was much quieter than it is today. That was when the Great North Road still followed its traditional line a mile or so to the east. Today, the ancient route has been replaced by the A1 trunk road – a much busier route in these days of the infernal combustion engine – and of the close proximity of which the locals must constantly be only too well aware!

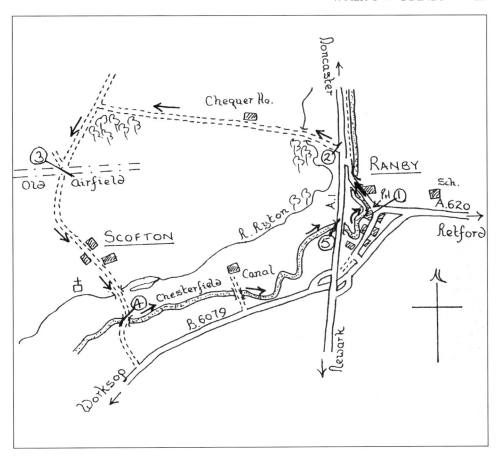

However, considering its situation, Ranby is still a surprisingly secluded backwater, easily passed by – which unless, perhaps, you happen to be the landlord of the excellent local inn, is to its advantage. The few people who do stray here soon forget the sound of the traffic in the greater enjoyment of the pretty gardens, the wildfowl and the pleasure craft along the winding course of the Chesterfield Canal.

This walk is in two distinct sections. After crossing the busy main road, we follow quiet country lanes, going over the site of a former airfield to reach the even more secluded village of Scofton. Here, we join the Chesterfield Canal and follow the towpath back to Ranby.

THE WALK
❶ Follow Blyth Road to its junction with the A1 and cross over. Remember that this is a very busy and fast road, and extreme care is essential in crossing. There being a dual carriageway is a great help, but do make sure the road is clear before moving.

The ford at Scofton.

Safely over, turn right and then left onto the (private) side road.

❷   Through the gate, continue straight ahead, following Thievesdale Lane and passing the buildings of Chequer House Farm. The lane follows a perfectly straight line, to reach a T-junction after passing a fine wood – Coachroad Plantation.

Turn left, and continue ahead, still following a metalled lane. If, as is likely, you find the hard road tedious, you will probably get along better by using the grass verge which, here and on Thievesdale Lane, is good and wide.

FOOD and DRINK

The only available watering hole in Ranby is the Chequers Inn, on the corner of Blyth Road. The large and comfortable lounge-cum-bar is clearly made up of several separate rooms which have been knocked into one. And there is a pleasant canalside beer garden where the wildlife and passing pleasure craft can be enjoyed. A staggering choice of food is offered for your delectation, both on the menu and on the daily specials board. The superb Lock Gates Open Sandwich can be recommended as a meal in itself. Or, for the more ambitious, how about Black Pudding and Bacon for starters? Followed by Pie of the Day? Telephone: 01777 703329.

❸ Cross the broad concrete runway – all that remains of a former airfield — and continue to the pleasant hamlet of Scofton; little more than a farm and a few cottages, really. But it does have its own church, so perhaps 'hamlet' is not the correct title.

Cross the river Ryton. If you are feeling adventurous, you may prefer the ford to the adjacent bridge – but you may find it rather too deep! Continue ahead to the canal, bearing left to join the towpath.

❹ Follow the towpath. After passing Osberton Mill, on your left, the canal makes a wide sweep to the right and then left, passing close to the Worksop road, before negotiating a second, lesser double bend and heading north-east to reach, and pass beneath, the main road.

❺ Continue beside the canal, which follows a winding course from here back to the village street. This is perhaps the best piece of the walk, with plenty of wildfowl, several attractive gardens opening directly onto the canalside opposite, and the back view of the Chequers Inn – sadly not accessible from here. So, if you are thirsty, it is time to break into a trot!

PLACES of INTEREST

Clumber Park, the Regional Headquarters of the National Trust, lies off the A614 to the south, between Ollerton and the A1 junction. The park is open to the public all year during daylight hours. Various features, which include a walled garden, Victorian apiary, fig house, vineries, orchard and garden tools exhibition are open to visitors at weekends from April to September. Enquiries, regarding opening hours, special events and so on, to the Estate Office (telephone: 01909 476592). **Hodsock Priory Gardens** near Blyth, to the north, are open on bank holiday weekends (Sunday and Monday) and certain weekdays in summer. The gardens are also open during the spring, when the snowdrops are spectacular. Telephone: 01909 591204.

WALESBY

Length: 7 miles

Getting there: From the A614 (Nottingham-Doncaster) road, an eastward turning 2 miles north of the Ollerton roundabout is signposted for Walesby (2 miles).

Public transport: Stagecoach East Midlands route 15 between Mansfield, Ollerton and Walesby, regular daily service; Roadcar route 34/35 (Retford, Tuxford and New Ollerton) operates six journeys daily, Monday to Saturday, calling at Walesby.

Parking: There is ample roadside parking space along Main Street, which is free from through traffic.

Maps: OS Landranger 120 Mansfield and Worksop; Explorer 28 Sherwood Forest (GR 684707).

Walesby might seem an unremarkable village, lying as it does away from the busy traffic stream, a couple of miles or so from the bigger ex-mining town of New Ollerton. Surrounded by fields and woods, this is still essentially a rural community, despite the fact that most of the locals commute to work.

But Walesby is no backwater. For close by is the nationally renowned Walesby

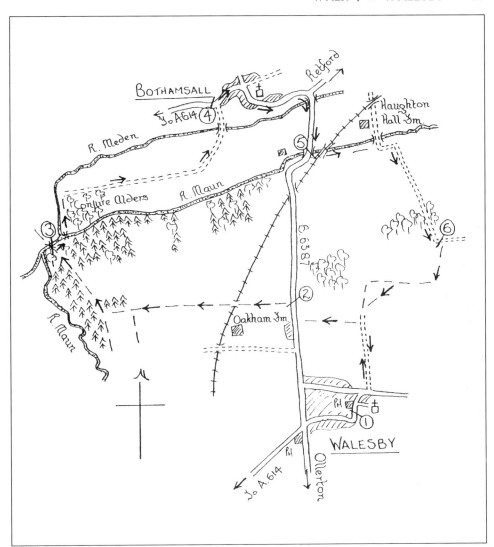

Forest Scout Camp. Not to mention the World of Robin Hood, just up the road towards Retford.

This is a walk of great variety and interest, passing close by the Scout Camp, but without disturbing the campers. A delightful forest walk brings us to the curiously named Conjure Alders, close to where the Maun and the Meden, like faithless lovers, unite and divide. Then to the village of Bothamsall, with its ancient motte, before returning over the prairies to Walesby.

The village of Bothamsall visited on the walk.

THE WALK

❶ Follow Main Street out to Tuxford Road and turn right, then go left onto Green Lane, continuing north and entering open country. After passing beneath an overhead power line, turn left again, following the line of the Robin Hood Way, beside the hedge, to the B6387 road. Turn right.

❷ Leave the road again, via a footpath on the left, by the 'no speed limit' sign. Pass the poultry houses and cross the railway (mineral line) bridge, continuing ahead on the left of the hedge. Keep the same direction through the woods, skirting the perimeter of the Scout Camp.

Turn right, following a clear, broad track over Blackcliffe Hill, and bearing left at a junction of paths to follow the bridleway arrows through to a footbridge over the river Maun.

❸ Do not cross this footbridge, but turn right along the nearside of the river, passing a weir, to reach a second footbridge. Along this section of the walk we find the most unusual circumstance of two rivers — the Maun and the Meden — uniting to form one; and immediately parting company again. There used to be a ford in this vicinity where the King's Highway — one of the oldest roads in the county — crossed the river.

Cross this bridge (over the Maun) and continue along the lush green bank of the Meden.

At the end of the wood turn right, away from the river, following a gravelled farm lane. Keep to the track as it swings left, continuing over the Meden bridge to join the road in Bothamsall village. As you approach the road, note the wooded hillock to the left, ahead of you. This is Bothamsall Castle — an ancient motte.

❹　Turn right and follow the road through Bothamsall, passing the church with its impressive tower, continuing to the far end of the village, and on to the junction with the B6387.

PLACES of INTEREST

The **World of Robin Hood**, off the B6387 at Haughton, about 1 1/2 miles north of Walesby. Adventure in sound and vision brings medieval history to life, with a journey through the crusades and a visit to a very real medieval market place. Open from 10.30 am to 5 pm, Easter to October; in winter, telephone 01623 860210 for opening times.

Turn right (as for Walesby) and follow the road for nearly 1/2 mile. Before reaching the bend (a fast and dangerous one), cross over to the left of the road.

❺　On the bend, turn left through the car park, following the farm track and passing under the railway bridge; keep straight forward beside the river Maun.

Turn right opposite Haughton Hall Farm, following the farm track left and right away from the river. After passing through a belt of woodland, the track feeds into a green lane.

❻　Bend left with the lane, leaving almost immediately via a stile on the right, and following the succeeding footpath on the right of the hedge. Turn right at the end of the field, still keeping the hedge on your left. After a time, the hedge transfers to the right, and the footpath, according to the OS map, crosses the field diagonally left. When surveyed, however, there was no sign of the path on this line, the indications being that the accepted route continued ahead, beside the hedge. Either way, turn left after crossing, continuing with the track to reach Green Lane, and retracing your outward route back to Walesby.

FOOD and DRINK

You will find a friendly welcome at the Red Lion on Main Street. The menu is economically priced and of wide variety. Or, if you prefer a 'lite bite', you can settle for a jacket potato or freshly made sandwich. And the kiddies will love the 'Rumbletums' selection. Opening hours are rather unusual here: 4 pm to 11 pm Monday to Thursday, 2 pm to 11 pm on Friday. Weekend hours are more traditional. Telephone: 01623 861193. Another good stopover (a little off route, but well worth the diversion) is the Carpenter's Arms on the corner of Boughton Road and Brake Road. This is the only pub I know that advertises a welcome to Scouts — the more mature ones, of course! There is a fully comprehensive menu here, and traditional hours operate. Telephone: 01623 860716. And, a little way along Brake Road, at Sandhurst Nurseries, the Thirsty Gardener Cafe offers a splendid selection, seven days a week. Telephone: 01623 836528. If you require the makings of a picnic, you should find all you need at the well-stocked post office/general store, in the village.

SOUTH CLIFTON

Length: 4 miles

Getting there: Take the A1133 (Newark-Gainsborough) road. The turning for South Clifton is a little over 2 miles south of the junction with the A57 at Newton on Trent.

Public transport: Travelwright

service 67 (Newark-Collingham-Harby) calls at South and North Clifton, six journeys daily, Monday to Saturday only.

Parking: High Street or Trent Lane, South Clifton (on-

street parking).

Maps: OS Landranger 121 Lincoln and surrounding area; Pathfinder 764 Lincoln and Saxilby (GR 821701).

North and South Clifton are twin villages, lying just to the east of the river in the peaceful flat borderlands of Lincolnshire. But although the two villages are separated by a little over a mile of quiet country lane, they are, in essence, one. For the shared church and school are situated on a 'jack-knife' bend, midway between the two.

The river — overlooked on its opposite bank by High Marnham Power Station — is a major attraction of both villages, and

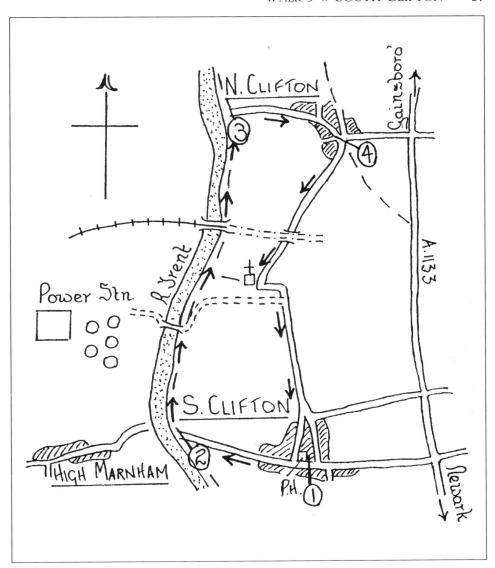

popular with anglers, water-skiers and boaters — and, of course, walkers! But it has not always been a peaceful waterway, for it had to be called to order, with the construction of a new flood bank, after the disastrous floods of 1947.

On this walk, a pleasant, easy stroll takes us down Trent Lane to the riverside, where we continue northwards, enjoying the riparian delights, to reach Trent Lane's northern counterpart. In North Clifton there is the opportunity to visit a beautiful

The Japanese Garden, North Clifton.

and inspiring Japanese garden — and enjoy, perhaps, a cup of tea or coffee — before returning along the road to South Clifton.

THE WALK

❶ Follow Trent Lane (west) out of the village, over the flood bank and down to the river. The power station on the opposite side of the river is High Marnham, one of several similar features to be found up and down the Trent valley.

❷ Turn right along the riverside, passing

beneath a suspension bridge. This is not a public bridge, but is provided specifically as

---

FOOD and DRINK

The Red Lion Inn in South Clifton's High Street is a smart, nicely modernised village pub, offering a friendly welcome and a wide range of bar food: full meals and snacks, salads and sandwiches. Food is served every lunchtime, also in the evening, except Monday and Tuesday — although parties can be accommodated on either of these days by prior arrangement. Sunday lunches are also available here. Telephone: 01522 778660.

an access point for power station employees. A gate beyond the bridge carries a 'private' notice — but this refers to the fishing rights. The footpath is part of the Trent Valley Way, and open to the public.

Continue, passing beneath a railway viaduct. This is now redundant — although the track appears still to be in place on the other side of the river, as far as the power station. Pass a warning notice (sunken island) and carry on to Trent Lane, North Clifton.

❸ Follow Trent Lane to the village. While here, you are recommended to spend a while at the Pureland Japanese Garden. This beautiful spot was created out of a level field by the Buddhist monk Maitreya, who still operates a meditation centre here. It is difficult to believe that, prior to creating the garden, Maitreya had no previous gardening knowledge or experience.

PLACES of INTEREST

Pureland Relaxation and Meditation Centre, and Japanese Garden in North Clifton. The garden is open from April to October: Tuesday to Saturday from 12.30 pm to 5.30 pm, Sundays and bank holidays from 10.30 am to 5.30 pm. There is a charge for admission. For further details, including information about meditation sessions, telephone 01777 228567.

---

❹ Follow High Street through the village, keeping straight on past Hall Farm, for South Clifton. There is a scrappy gravel path to the left of the road, although the roadway is not heavily used and should be a safe option provided you keep to the right. Pass the parish church and the school building and continue back to South Clifton.

LAXTON

Length: 5 miles

Getting there: From the Ollerton roundabout on the A614 road, follow the A6075 east through New Ollerton and Boughton. Where the main road bends sharp left for Kirton, keep straight forward on the unclassified side road, passing beneath the railway bridge and continuing through to Laxton.

The walk commences at the Visitor Centre, by the Dovecote Inn, at the eastern end of the village.

Public transport: Roadcar routes 34 and 35 Retford-Tuxford-New Ollerton, six journeys each way, Monday to Saturday.

Parking: Laxton Visitor Centre (behind the Dovecote Inn).

Maps: OS Landranger 120 Mansfield and Worksop; Pathfinder 780 Ollerton (GR 724671).

One of the most fascinating villages in the county, Laxton is the only place in England where the medieval three-field system still survives intact. West Field, South Field and Mill Field, covering a total of 483 acres, are still unfenced, and the Court Leet still meets, in the Dovecote Inn in November each year, to administer the

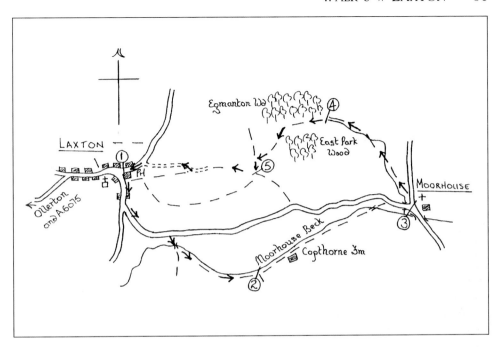

annual leases. The village is dominated by the impressive 13th-century parish church of St Michael, itself worth a visit while you are here, and other features of local interest include the village pinfold, close by the inn, and one of the best preserved motte and baileys in the country.

Our outward journey follows the northern edge of South Field, beside the

Moorhouse Beck, to reach the tiny hamlet of Moorhouse; remarkable for its intriguing 'church in a field'. We return via pleasant fieldpaths, negotiating stiles of diverse quality and difficulty, and skirting the edge of Egmanton Wood.

THE WALK

❶ Turn left outside the pub, following the Kneesall road past the pinfold. Left again at the turning for Moorhouse, continuing along this secondary road. Beyond the 'no limit' sign, take the waymarked track on the right, passing to the right of an electric pylon. Cross a stream and turn left, now following a pleasant green way, with the broad expanse of the South Field on your right and Moorhouse Beck on your left.

FOOD and DRINK

The obvious (and only) genuine watering hole in Laxton is the Dovecote Inn. This is a busy and popular house with a cosy and friendly atmosphere, where families are manifestly welcome. There is a full range of meals and snacks, or sandwiches. Telephone: 01777 871586. If you prefer to make up your own picnic, the little village post office should be able to help.

Moorhouse and its 'church in a field'.

❷   Where the track bends right, keep straight ahead, through the hedge, still following the beck along the edge of the field and passing Copthorne Farm. Cross a footbridge over the beck and follow the hedge up to the road. Turn right, to Moorhouse.

❸   Turn left at the road junction, noting the attractive church, in the field by Church Farm. The church can be reached via a hand-gate (waymarked) but, if you wish to see inside, you will need to obtain the key from the farm.

Returning to the road, turn right, then

go left over a stile opposite Sunnyside Cottage. Keep straight ahead in the first field, bearing right at a footpath arrow to follow the right bank of a stream. After passing to the left of a pylon, cross a stile on the left, bearing right over the next field to reach a second stile, beside a tree. Care is required in negotiating the stiles on this section of the route, many of which are topped with barbed wire and at least one is in poor condition. Turn left after crossing this stile and follow the hedge over the next two fields.

❹ Cross the stile on your left and continue right, beside Egmanton Wood and with East Park Wood on your left. Cross an excellent footbridge and turn half-

---

PLACES of INTEREST

Laxton Visitor Centre (adjacent to the Dovecote Inn) is open daily, from 10 am to 8 pm. Admission is free, but donations are welcome. Telephone: 01777 871586.

---

left across the next field, continuing via the fieldpath over the following two fields. Part-way over the second of these, turn left onto the intersecting path and continue to the end of the field.

❺ Pass through the gate and turn right along the farm track, continuing ahead, back to Laxton. A footpath on the left, part-way along, offers an alternative route back, via the pinfold.

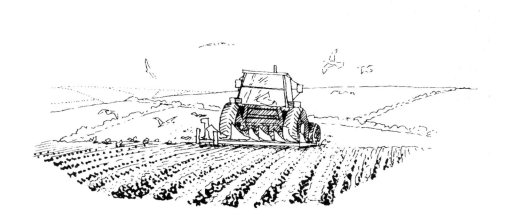

WELLOW

Length: 4½ or 5½ miles

Getting there: Wellow lies on the A616 (Sheffield-Newark) road, about 1½ miles south-east of Ollerton. If coming from the Nottingham direction, leave the A614 at the Rufford turning; first right after the entrance to Rufford Country Park. Wellow is about 2 miles from here.

Public transport: Stagecoach East Midlands route 13: Mansfield-Ollerton-Wellow provides a regular service throughout the week, including Sundays.

Parking: The best place to park, in the village, is on the side road to the west of the green — having due regard, of course, for the residents of the road. Access is from Eakring Road end only. Parking space is also available (ostensibly for anglers), outside the village, by Wellow Dam.

Maps: OS Landranger 120 Mansfield and Worksop; OS Explorer 28 Sherwood Forest (GR 670661).

Wellow is a 'conservation' village, and planning is strictly controlled, preventing the developmental blight so often seen elsewhere. As a result, the heart of the village remains totally unspoilt, with a maypole on the village green, and time-

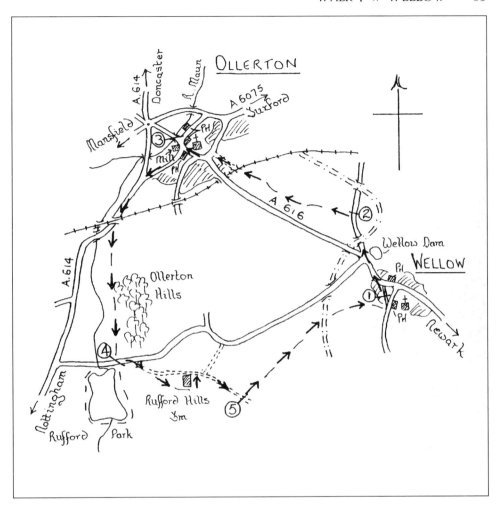

mellowed dwellings of red brick and pantiles all around.

This, unusually, was a fortified village — to protect the villagers and their livestock, we are told, from the unwelcome attentions of neighbours — and the remains of the ancient earthworks, and the Gorge Dyke are still to be seen. The writer has been told that a previous village lies beneath the Green and that, if you put

your ear to the ground there, you can still hear the sound of children at play. A wind-up? Perhaps, but a nice tale!

This is a walk in three distinct stages — with an optional fourth stage thrown in for good measure. The first stage takes us to the neighbouring village of Old Ollerton; like Wellow a totally unspoilt oasis. After brief contact with the main A614 road, a fine bridleway leads over the Ollerton Hills

Ollerton and its mill stream.

to Rufford, where the delights of Rufford Country Park, with its charming lake, beckon. The walk concludes with the traverse of Rufford Hills, over wide arable fields, back to Wellow.

THE WALK

❶ Join the A616 and turn left, following the road round the bend and past Wellow Dam — an attractive amenity pool, popular with anglers. Turn right onto the unclassified Boughton road and continue, passing beneath the railway bridge.

❷ Turn left into a side road (called, confusingly, Wellow Green), leaving again via a footpath on the right, and following the foot of a former colliery spoil tip — now in the course of restoration and landscaping. Keep to the same general line (save for a couple of double bends), as indicated by the guide posts. Pass a caravan site and cross a bridge over the railway, continuing via a gravel track to Wellow Road. Turn left; and right again to reach Ollerton old village.

Ollerton is a charming, unspoilt old-world village, happily isolated from traffic and industry by the diversion of the main Doncaster road and the development of the neighbouring mining town of New Ollerton. The river Maun runs through the centre of the village and, close by, Ollerton Watermill is well worth a visit.

❸ Leave Ollerton via Station Road, joining the A614 and continuing towards Nottingham. After passing beneath the railway bridge, branch left onto the way-marked green lane. A good track leads past Ollerton Hills woods, to meet the road at Rufford.

The 'official' route turns left here for Wellow. But before that, you are recommended to continue over the road, and follow the path around Rufford Park Lake — and, perhaps, call in at the Rufford Mill Centre and shop. This will add no more than a mile to your total walk.

❹ From the Ollerton path, turn left and follow the road as far as the entrance to Rufford Golf Centre. Take the waymarked footpath, half right, over the stile beside the farm gate (Rufford Hills Farm). This is a

PLACES of INTEREST

Situated in the centre of Ollerton, the **Ollerton Watermill** is the only working watermill in Nottinghamshire, and houses a visitor centre and teashop. The visitor centre is open from April to September, Sunday afternoons and Bank Holidays, from 12 noon until 5 pm. Group visits or other times by arrangement. Telephone: 01623 822469/ 824094. **Rufford Country Park** is an area of woodland and parkland which contains the remains of the 12th-century Rufford Cistercian Abbey. There is an exhibition telling the history of the abbey and of its conversion to a country house. The lake is home to a variety of wildlife, and the gardens are an added attraction. Refreshments and meals are provided at the Coach House and Buttery, and there is a craft shop and gallery. Admission is free, but there is a parking charge at weekends and Bank Holidays/ school holidays, in summer. The park is open daily till dusk. For other details, telephone: 01623 824153.

FOOD and DRINK

There is no shortage of refreshment houses on the route of this walk, with two pubs in Wellow itself, and three in Ollerton old village; all providing good food and drink. But star billing must go to the teashop attached to Ollerton Mill. The food, decor and service here are second to none. A varied and excellent menu covers both lunches and teas, at reasonable prices. Telephone: 01623 824094/ 822469.

Alternative food-stops in Ollerton are the White Hart, on Station Road (telephone: 01623 822410); the Snooty Fox, on Main Street (telephone: 01623 823073); and the Hop Pole Hotel, on Church Street (telephone: 01623 822573).

And Wellow village has the Olde Red Lion, on Eakring Road (telephone: 01623 861000) and the Durham Ox, on Newark Road (telephone: 01623 861026).

private road, but a public right of way on foot. As you approach the farm, bear right along the hedge-side, bypassing the farm buildings. Turn left with the hedge-line at a guide-post, cross a stile and rejoin the farm road, turning right.

Where the road bends left, take the track on the right, continuing up the rise until you reach a guide-post, pointing left.

❺   Turn left. The path from here is over vast arable fields and, depending on the state of the crops (i.e. if not many walkers have preceded you!) the route may not be too obvious. There is a very helpful, solitary tree in the centre of this first field, directly on the line of the path, so you should not go wrong. In the second field, bear slightly left of this line, keeping the highest ground on your right. This is, in fact, the highest ground on the walk, with splendid views over the surrounding countryside.

Cross a (redundant) railway cutting — there are 70-odd steps down and the same out again. Note also that the land on either side of the cutting is horse-gallops — so look out! Cross a high, and tricky stile, and continue over the fields, back to Wellow.

TEVERSAL

Length: 3½ miles

Getting there: Turn off the B6014 (Mansfield-Matlock) road west of Stanton Hill, at the 'Teversal Trails' sign. Continue along Carnarvon Street to the Visitor Centre car park.

Public transport: Trent/ Stagecoach service 141 Clay Cross-Mansfield-Nottingham, daily service; Trent service 142 Mansfield-Sutton-Teversal, daily service (not Sundays).

Parking: There is limited space for roadside parking in the old village, opposite the church. But it is sensible to use the Visitor Centre car park at the top of Carnarvon Street.

Maps: OS Landranger 120 Mansfield and Worksop; OS Pathfinder 779 Mansfield North (GR 479614).

Teversal has been described as an oasis in an industrial wilderness. This was a particularly apt description a few years ago when there were two pits within a mile of the old village, which was itself completely encircled by mineral railway lines yet still retained its traditional rural charm.

Today, both pits — Silverhill and Teversal — have gone, their sites reclaimed and the old mineral lines converted to

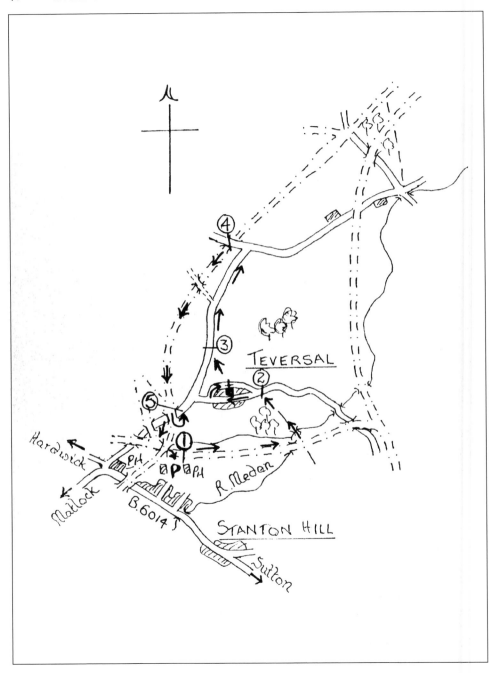

A bridge over the river Meden.

cycle/walkways. The village itself is as pretty as any, with an ancient manor house and church and attractive stone cottages. This is the area immortalised by D.H. Lawrence in *Lady Chatterley's Lover* — and the Manor itself was used in that work as the model for 'Wragby Hall'.

With the conversion of the former railway tracks, the country-goer has inherited a splendid network of recreational ways to supplement the traditional footpaths of the district. This short walk makes full use of both footpath and trail, much of the time following sections of the 'Lady Chatterley Trail' — a 6 mile tour of the district associated with Lawrence's shady lady. The footpaths are excellent and well-trodden and have first-class stiles, and much of the way — along the trails at any rate — is negotiable by wheelchair.

The route passes through the old village, providing an opportunity to visit the ancient church and admire the Manor and cottages.

THE WALK

❶ Join the Teversal Trail (via the 'Coal Garden') and turn right. Follow for a long ½ mile, then leave by a waymarked footpath on the left, crossing the infant river Meden and continuing over the fields to Old Teversal.

❷ Turn left to follow the back lane, passing Manor Farm. Pass through the gates and continue with the Manor on your left and St Katherine's church on the right. Beyond the church, the road turns right to reach the village street via a gate; alternatively, a footpath straight ahead also leads to the village street, at the western end of the village. You may take either route — and turn right at the road.

Opposite the church, a waymark points the way over a field, and a clear footpath

---

PLACES of INTEREST

Hardwick Hall, the celebrated home of Bess of Hardwick and now a National Trust property (GR 462633), lies to the east of the M1, just a few miles from Teversal, and can be reached via the minor road from Fackley (by the Carnarvon Arms) to Stainsby. The Country Park is open all year, dawn to dusk; the Hall and gardens are open from the end of March to the beginning of November, the Hall from Wednesday to Sunday and Bank Holiday Monday (but not Good Friday), 12.30 pm to 5 pm, the gardens daily, 12 noon to 5.30 pm. Telephone: 01246 850430.

---

will bring you out on the Pleasley road.

❸ Turn right along the road. Some way along, a track on the left leads to Norwood Lodge — associated with Gamekeeper Mellors, the eponymous hero of *Lady Chatterley's Lover*. This track may be used to reach the return route of the Teversal Trail, but access to the track itself is tricky, and it is better to continue ahead for the present.

Walk along the road to its junction with Newbound Lane and turn left, to join the former railway track a little way along.

❹ Descend left to join the trail, and follow to the outskirts of Teversal, descending here as directed to join a road.

❺ Turn left to pass under the bridge, then left again onto a fieldpath — involving a minor stream crossing. Turn left once more on reaching the southern section of the trail, passing beneath the bridge, and return to the Visitor Centre car park.

FOOD and DRINK

The Visitor Centre provides a selection of snacks (tea, coffee, pasties, cakes and sundries) in a pleasant and friendly atmosphere. Children, dogs and muddy boots are welcome. And you are free to browse around the exhibits at the same time. Telephone: 01623 442021. If you prefer something more substantial to eat, the Teversal Grange Country Inn (formerly the Miners' Welfare) will be found on the opposite side of the car park. Telephone: 01623 441017. A little off the route at Fackley, where the B6014 bends left for Huthwaite, is the Carnarvon Arms — said to be the most haunted inn in Nottinghamshire. Telephone: 01623 559676.

CAUNTON

Length: 4½ miles

<table>
<tr><td>

Getting there: Caunton is situated just off (north side of) the A616 (Newark-Ollerton) road, about 6 miles north-west of Newark.

Public transport: Travelwright, Newark, service 32 calls at Caunton; five

</td><td>

journeys daily, Monday to Saturday only.

Parking: Apart from the car parks of either of the two pubs (bona fide customers only, subject to verbal permission), there is a certain amount of parking space

</td><td>

alongside some of the village roads.

Maps: OS Landranger 120 Mansfield and Worksop; Pathfinder 780 Ollerton and 796 Newark-on-Trent West (GR 745600).

</td></tr>
</table>

In a county long noted for its roses, one of the most celebrated names is that of Samuel Reynolds Hole who, before serving as Dean of Rochester, was vicar and squire of Caunton. The most famous of all amateur rosarians, he recorded in 1851 that he had 1,027 trees, of over 400 different varieties.

There was a tradition in Caunton known as the 'Rang-Tang', which should perhaps

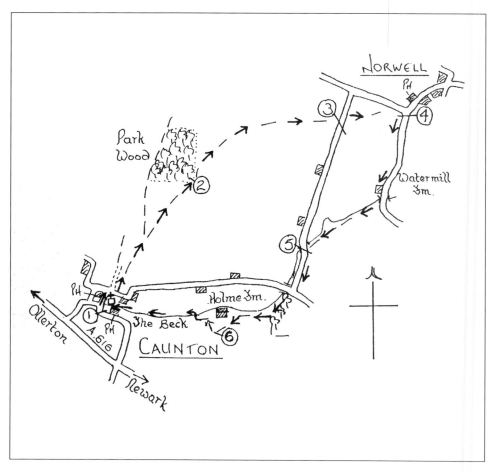

be adopted more generally today, for shaming men who persistently beat or abused their wives and children. The custom was for a band of performers with makeshift instruments (kettles, fire shovels and suchlike) to serenade the culprit, beneath his window, late at night. After three nights of this, the offender was burnt in effigy and the church bell tolled.

Caunton today is a quiet but pleasant village, with a pretty brook (The Beck) and few of the less welcome trappings of 20th-

century life.

The route of this walk crosses fertile arable fields, passing close by Park Wood, to reach the neighbouring village of Norwell. Usually pronounced 'Norral', the name is a corruption of North Well — the counterpart of Southwell.

We do not linger long in Norwell (unless to patronise the local inn), but return to Caunton via Mill Bridge, with the climax of the walk a delightful beckside stroll past Caunton church, back to the village.

The path alongside Caunton beck.

THE WALK

❶ Follow the main street northwards past the church, turning right onto Norwell Road and then taking the waymarked bridlepath on the left, crossing a paddock. Bear right in the next field, and again at a second intersection, making for the right-hand extremity of Park Wood.

❷ Walk along the edge of the wood to a gap on the left and a blocked-off stile. Turn your back on the stile and follow the path across the open field. Cross a footbridge and continue, heading for a distant overhead power line. Pass beneath it, and continue to the road.

❸ Turn left for a short distance only, leaving again by a stile on the right, beside a field gate. Follow the hedge on your left, then go diagonally left over the next field. Through a gate, continue to Norwell village street. Turn right, passing Schoolhouse Farm and on to the road junction, almost opposite the Plough Inn, where a welcome seat offers the chance of a rest.

❹ Turn right, and follow the lane past Watermill Farm and over Mill Bridge. Turn off through a gateway on the right — there is no waymark or guidepost evident here, but a faint path should be visible to the left of the beck. Follow this for the full length of a long field, to a stile at the top. Continue ahead over the fields to reach the road, beside a bridge over the beck.

❺ Turn left and follow the road to a

T-junction. Cross straight over and continue along the waymarked track. After a field gate, a footpath waymark will be seen confirming the route of the track you are presently using — forward and back along the wooded track.

Ignoring the arrowed directions, turn right over a makeshift stile and cross the field, to join the hedge and follow it to a footbridge. Cross over and turn left, following the hedgeside path over a series of stiles and passing to the left of Holme Farm.

❻   Past the farm, double back right across the field to arrive at, and cross, another makeshift stile. Continue along the fieldside to another footbridge. Cross, and follow The Beck back to Caunton, bearing in mind that the way passes through the

grounds of several private residences — proceed with courtesy!

FARNSFIELD

Length: 6½ or 7 miles

Getting there: From the A614 (Nottingham-Doncaster) road just south of its junction with the A617, turn off east at the White Post roundabout, onto the unclassified Rainworth-Southwell road. Farnsfield is just over a mile on along here.

Public transport: Farnsfield is served by Stagecoach East Midlands, with frequent services (Newark-Southwell-Mansfield, Nottingham-Worksop, and Nottingham-Retford).

Parking: Farnsfield main street is narrowish along much of its length. The best area for parking is at the western end, in the vicinity of the church.

Maps: OS Landranger 120 Mansfield and Worksop; Explorer 28 Sherwood Forest (GR 646666).

Farnsfield, one of Nottinghamshire's bigger villages lies in the heart of the ancient forest of Sherwood. There are traces of ancient peoples hereabouts, amid rolling hills and old woodlands. The village was the birthplace (in 1819) of Augustus Gregory, who explored the interior of Australia and was known as the protector of the Aborigines.

A feature of the village is the Southwell

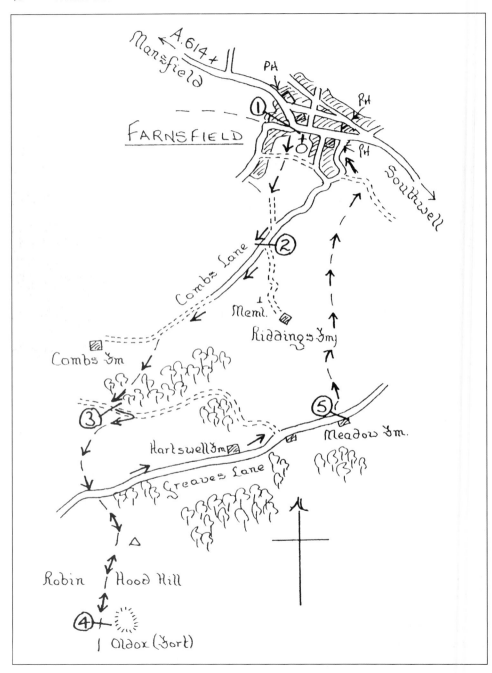

Memorial to the crew of a Halifax bomber which crashed nearby.

Trail, formerly a section of the Mansfield to Southwell railway line and now a popular recreational route.

The walk takes us up onto the wooded hills to the south of Farnsfield. The predominance of oak trees along the lanes and byways — so different from the more familiar 20th-century pinewood forestry — reminds us that this is true Sherwood country. Appropriately, the high point of the walk — in more ways than one — is Robin Hood Hill, close to the Iron Age Oldox hillfort.

An optional diversion along the way, which adds a total of ¹/₄ mile to the walk, leads to a moving reminder of a wartime aerial tragedy.

THE WALK

❶   Leave Main Street via Blidworth Road, turning left immediately onto Church Side and bearing right to follow the wallside footway. Cross a road and follow the clearly defined bridleway over two fields, continuing via an overgrown green lane to Combs Lane. Turn right along the metalled roadway.

Soon after you have joined this road, a turning on the left leads to Riddings Farm and the Halifax Bomber Memorial — fully deserving a diversion of ¹/₄ mile and a few minutes of your time.

The memorial commemorates the crash of Halifax bomber MZ519 on land belonging to Riddings Farm, on 6 July 1944, while returning from a bombing mission against a V1 rocket site. The whole crew were killed. The memorial stone was erected 50 years later, on a site which incorporates a copse of trees, including seven Nottinghamshire oaks (one per crew member) and two red maples. These last were a gift from Canada, recording the fact that one crew member was a Canadian. The people of Farnsfield have undertaken to maintain the site in perpetuity.

❷ Returning to Combs Lane, continue to the left (or go straight on if you have not diverted to the memorial) as the way reverts to a farm track. Short of Combs Farm, bear left to cross the fields on a diagonal line, making for Combs Wood.

Inside the wood, follow the waymarked route right and left and ascend to a stile. Cross and turn left, following the edge of the field to a guidepost and a gravel lane.

❸ Turn left along the lane, passing an opening on the right but keeping an eye open for a path, also on the right but without a waymark, leading through the hedge. Pass through and double back,

---

FOOD and DRINK

There are three pubs in Farnsfield village, all of which provide bar food. The Plough, at the eastern end of Main Street (telephone: 01623 882265) is the oldest, a homely and traditional village inn with beams, brasses and an open fireplace. The others are the Warwick Arms, also on Main Street (telephone: 01623 882360) and the Red Lion, at the western end of the village, on Mansfield Road (telephone: 01623 882304). The village is well provided with shops for snack materials.

PLACES of INTEREST

A mile or so to the west of Farnsfield, near the White Post roundabout, the **Wonderland Pleasure Park** offers a glorious variety of entertainment for all the family, in 30 acres of superb parkland. It includes a nine hole golf course (and crazy golf), a giant sandpit, a huge bouncy castle — and much else. Telephone: 01623 882773. In the same area, the **White Post Modern Farm Centre** is a working farm with displays and exhibitions, where visitors can meet over 4,000 animals of all kinds (even llamas!). There are picnic sites and indoor areas, including a reptile house, as well as a gift shop and tea rooms. Telephone: 01623 882977.

---

keeping the hedge on your right. At the end of the second field, turn left. Then go right, as waymarked, at a gap, following a clear track towards a prominent oak tree.

On reaching the tree, pause to enjoy the wide views over to the west before turning left, as directed by the adjacent guidepost, and following the fieldpath through to Greaves Lane.

Cross the road and continue, following the gravelled farm lane. Where the track swings left, turn off right, crossing the field to reach Loath Hill Wood. Keep to the path along the right-hand side of the wood, crossing a stile at the end and carrying on beside the fence, with Robin Hood Hill on your left. An easy ascent to the top of the hill will reward you with more fine, wide views over the surrounding countryside. A little way to the south of here, on private land, is the ancient Oldox hillfort.

❹ Descend to rejoin the footpath, re-turning to Greaves Lane and turning right along the road. Here, as elsewhere on the route, note the predominance of oak trees in the fields and woods and along the roadside, a clear reminder of the area's history as a part of Sherwood Forest.

❺ After passing Hartswell Farm and Wood Farm, turn left through a field gate opposite Meadow Farm, following a lightly used track. Turn right after a little way, to follow the edge of the field round and go through the hedge, continuing on the right of the hedge, beneath a telephone line. At the top of the field, continue right and left, dog-leg fashion, resuming your former line, now on the left of the hedge.

Keep straight forward now, following the waymarked path back to Farnsfield.

SELSTON

Length: 3½ miles

Getting there: From Nottingham, via the A610 to Nuthall roundabout, and thence by the B600. If coming from the Mansfield direction, follow the A38 and the B6018, to join the B600 at Selston and head towards Alfreton. In both cases, turn off right at the western end of Selston (Selston Green) onto Church Lane.

Public transport: Trent Buses operate a half-hourly service (route R12) between Alfreton, Eastwood and Nottingham, from Monday to Saturday. An hourly service (Dunn Line, route 12) runs on Sundays between Alfreton and Eastwood only. Both services pass along the B600 at Selston.

Parking: Church Lane, Selston Green; opposite or adjacent to the parish church (roadside).

Maps: OS Landranger 120 Mansfield and Worksop; Pathfinder 795 Sutton in Ashfield (GR 458533).

Little remains today of the original village of Selston, which stood around the church on the hilltop overlooking the Erewash valley and the Derbyshire hills. The present settlement is a blend of traditional working-class and modern housing, mostly

Dan Boswell's memorial stone in the churchyard at Selston.

to the east of the church, where the mining village developed. The mines have all gone now — the last one closed in 1956. But this is still, basically, an industrial area. Coal was mined here from the 13th century, and ironstone mining and framework knitting have also contributed to the local economy. But do not be misled: there is some truly charming, rural 'green belt' countryside on Selston's doorstep. And the great D. H. Lawrence counted this area 'the country of my heart'.

After visiting the churchyard and admiring the view over to the west, where the Derbyshire hills beckon — for attention on another occasion! — and inspecting an intriguing memorial stone, we soon leave the houses behind on this walk, crossing the fieldpaths to the neighbouring hamlet of Lower Bagthorpe. Here, in this idyllic spot, it is difficult to imagine that we are still in the heart of the Nottinghamshire and Derbyshire coalfield. Nor, as we make our return journey, that we are passing over the actual sites of former pits. The scars are well healed.

THE WALK

❶ Before starting the walk, call in the churchyard. One of the gravestones here — so we are told — is that of Dan Boswell, the King of the Gipsies. The original stone is unrecognisable, the epitaph having been erased through the ravages of over a century of time. But a modern stone by the church tower bears a copy of the inscription.

Leaving the church, cross Church Lane and follow Desborough Road; turn right at the end, onto Lindley Street. Leave the road via a passageway on the left and follow the ensuing fieldpath through to Alfreton Road and the Bull and Butcher inn.

❷ Pass the inn, and the Jacksdale road junction. Cross Nottingham Road and join the footpath to the left of a house. Over a stile (overgrown when we came), cross the field and a farm track, skirting around to the left of Ashes Farm. The setting of the farm is delightful, with a large duck pond backed by ancient buildings, in a blend of red brick and grey stone.

Continue along a well-signed fieldpath, turning right to pass Home Farm. After crossing Bagthorpe Brook, branch left; then go right after crossing a stile, following the hedgeside up the hill to reach the road, by Wansley Hall Farm.

FOOD and DRINK

The Bull and Butcher on Alfreton Road is a roomy estate pub, providing pleasant service. There is a full and varied daily menu — including a special children's menu — and a range of daily specials is listed on the bar blackboards. Snacks and sandwiches are available throughout opening hours. Telephone: 01773 810591. The Shepherd's Rest at Lower Bagthorpe is a charming country pub around the halfway point of the walk, offering fine cask-conditioned ales and good home-cooked food. Telephone: 01773 810506.

PLACES of INTEREST

While in D.H. Lawrence country, why not make a day of it by visiting the author's **Birthplace Museum**, at 8a Victoria Street, Eastwood? This is 5 miles south of Selston, via the A608. For opening hours and charges, telephone 01773 763312. Between Selston and Eastwood, the **Brinsley Headstocks and picnic area** occupy the site of Brinsley Colliery, where Lawrence's father worked.

---

❸ Turn left along the road, descending to Lower Bagthorpe and the Shepherd's Rest inn. Leave the road here via a waymarked footpath between Manor Farm and the inn, continuing over the fields (ex-colliery lands) to Inkerman.

❹ Follow Inkerman Road north, soon leaving the road via an enclosed footpath on the left and descending to the outskirts of Selston. Cross an estate road and continue ahead, bearing right to meet, and cross, Nottingham Road and turn left.

❺ After passing Selston C of E School, turn right as indicated by the footpath sign. Follow the footway round to the right, crossing a stile and a footbridge and entering onto fields. Follow the hedge on your left, up the fields, to emerge onto Stoney Lane. Turn left and continue back to Church Lane.

CALVERTON

Length: 5 miles

Getting there: Via the A6097 (Fosse Way-Oxton) road. Leave the main road 1 mile north-west of Epperstone, following Moor Lane — signposted for Calverton. **Public transport:** Barton service 8 Nottingham-Arnold-Calverton, every 20/40 minutes, Monday to	Saturday; services 7 and 7a Nottingham-Woodborough-Calverton, hourly, Monday to Saturday; Barton/Pathfinder joint service 308 Nottingham-Arnold-Lambley-Calverton, two-hourly Sunday service. **Parking:** Alongside Main Street in Calverton; or in the	'shoppers' car park', St Wilfrid's Square (centre of the village, by the County Library). **Maps:** OS Landranger 129 Nottingham and Loughborough; Pathfinder 813 Carlton and Elston (GR 617493).

Calverton was the home of William Lee, the inventor, four centuries ago, of the stocking frame. His influence is still to be found here, in the stockingers' cottages, with their specially designed windows to maximise the available daylight, for Calverton has long been one of Nottinghamshire's main centres of the cottage hosiery

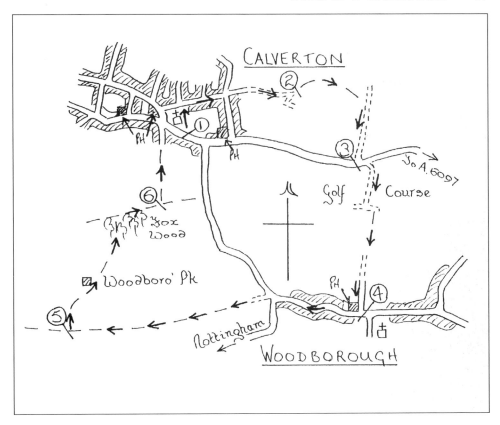

industry. There is also a long tradition in the district, both here and at neighbouring Woodborough, of market gardening. More recently, the local economy has relied heavily on the colliery which, despite the loss of most of the county's pits, still survives under private ownership.

The opening of the pit in 1952, and the development of a lot of private housing, has led to a seven-fold increase in the local population. But the old part of the village, around St Wilfrid's church and along Main Street, still retains its rural feel, and the quality of the walks, over the surrounding fields and hills, is second to none, with well-maintained footpaths and bridleways.

Starting from the village church, the walk passes through one of Calverton's more modern housing developments. But buildings are soon left behind as we cross open country in the direction of Epperstone and the Dover Beck. Turning south, we cross the hills to Woodborough, another of the county's most attractive villages, before taking the fieldpath route, via Woodborough Beck and Woodborough Park, to Fox Wood — the site of an ancient hillfort — and back to Calverton.

Calverton Framework Knitters' Cottages.

THE WALK

❶ Follow the footway to the right of the church to arrive at Crookdole Lane, and turn right. Keep on along here, crossing Park Road East and continuing past Carrington Lane, where the village is left behind.

❷ Where the lane bends sharp right, bear left along the waymarked footpath, following the side of a stream/ditch. Cross over via a bridge and continue on the opposite bank to reach a farm lane and turn right, following the lane to the road.

❸ Turn left, then go right by the golf course entrance, following the waymarked bridleway. Keep to the broad track, straight up the hill between the golf links. At a T-junction, turn left, then go right at a waymark arrow, continuing along an en-closed footpath. Pass a cemetery and descend to Woodborough, joining the main street by the Four Bells Inn.

❹ Turn right at the inn and follow Main

Street, bearing right at the road junction, onto the Calverton road. Cross straight over and join Westfield Lane. Follow the track between the houses and on over the fields, continuing with the fieldpath for about a mile, with the beck on your right.

❺ On meeting a farm track turn right, following the track through the gap in the hedge and on. Continue round to the right, passing the farm and bearing right to cross a stile into the next field. Cross the corner of this field and then go straight on over the next, up the hill, to reach Fox Wood.

Turn left inside the wood, following the footpath. The path passes through the site of an ancient hillfort, the double bank and ditch of which are still in existence. Some

---

PLACES of INTEREST

Calverton Framework Knitters' Cottages in Windles Square (not open to the public). **Calverton Folk Museum** in Main Street (open by appointment). Telephone: 0115 965 2836. **Patchings Farm Art Centre** in Oxton Road has a variety of aspects to interest the visitor. There are working art, craft and pottery studios, as well as art, gift and framing shops and a licensed restaurant, also over 50 acres of grounds where artists may paint and visitors may wander. Courses and tuition are available. Open daily, 9 am to 10.30 pm (gardens to 6 pm). Admission free — but a charge is payable for the gardens. Telephone: 0115 965 5308.

Roman pottery has been found on the site, although no excavation has been carried out.

At the northern perimeter of the wood, turn right along the track, continuing past the wood to a guidepost on the left.

❻ Turn left, and descend over the fields to Brickenell Road and Renals Way; and so back to Calverton.

FOOD and DRINK

There are three pubs in Calverton, the Admiral Rodney, on Main Street (corner of Manor Road), being particularly recommended. This clean and cheerful traditional village inn is attractive both inside and out, with flower baskets on the frontage. Good food is available daily, lunchtimes and evenings, in hearty portions without frills. Try the all-day breakfast! Telephone: 0115 965 2264. At the opposite end of the village, on Bonner Lane, the Gleaners provides bar food from Monday to Saturday, but only roast lunch on Sundays. Telephone: 0115 965 2226. Opposite the Gleaners, Catherine's Bakery can supply all the materials for a satisfying picnic: home-baked bread, filled rolls, home-made pies, cooked meat and cream cakes — as well as hot and cold drinks. Telephone: 0115 965 4347. And there is a sandwich bar in the centre of the village. Around its halfway point, in Woodborough village, the walk passes the Four Bells, a welcoming family pub with a kiddies' play area, offering daily lunches. Telephone: 0115 965 2214.

BLEASBY

Length: 5 miles

<table>
<tr><td>

Getting there: Follow the A612 from Nottingham or Southwell, turning off (east) at Thurgarton and continuing through Goverton and over the railway crossing.

Public transport: A regular train service between Nottingham, Newark and

</td><td>

Lincoln stops at Bleasby. Pathfinder buses between Southwell and Nottingham also serve Bleasby, Monday to Saturday only: route S3, three journeys daily; route S4, hourly service.

Parking: Roadside parking only — the most suitable

</td><td>

area appears to be along Gypsy Lane.

Maps: OS Landranger 120 Mansfield and Worksop; 129 Nottingham and Loughborough; Pathfinder 796 Newark-on-Trent West; 813 Carlton and Elston (GR 717496).

</td></tr>
</table>

Bleasby is a pretty village which has long been popular with Nottingham people, situated as it is so close to one of the most scenically attractive stretches of the river Trent. There is a local tradition that, in the

7th century, St Paulinus (sent by Augustine to evangelise the north) baptised his converts in the river here. In common with many other Trentside villages, Bleasby has been affected to some extent by the

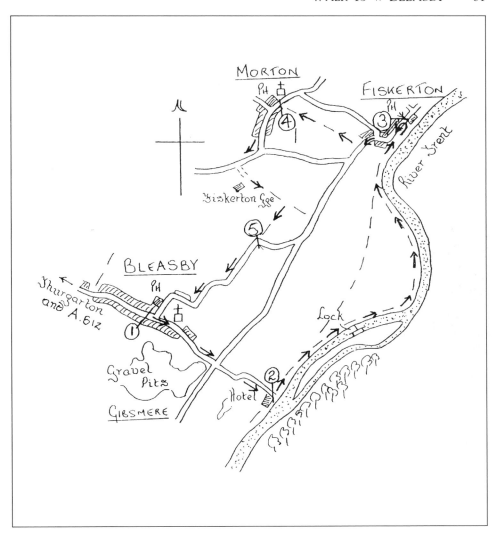

demand for gravel, but the most intrusive of the worked out pits have now been landscaped to form a valuable local amenity.

This is a lovely walk which could, if one is not careful, develop into a pub crawl (definitely not recommended!). Rather, take your time, particularly as you stroll along the riverside, enjoying the life of Nottinghamshire's most celebrated waterway: the anglers, the boats, the wildfowl. Not to mention the glorious views, over the river and across to the Trent Hills. The route visits two charming villages and the popular boating and caravanning centre of Hazelford Ferry. There is no ferry today, but the name persists.

Moorings at Hazelford Ferry.

THE WALK

❶ Follow the main street east, past the village church. At a crossroads, keep straight forward along the Hazelford Ferry road. This road is rather narrow and without a causeway. There are one or two bends and traffic can be heavy. So keep well in to the right of the road and take care. The road ends at Hazelford Ferry (the name is pronounced Hazzleford). The ferry no longer operates, but it lives on in the name of the inn. And there is plenty of life here still, with a caravan site, boat moorings and peaceful riverside walks in either direction.

❷ Turn left, following the Trent Valley

Way route downstream. Keep to the riverside path, past the weir and lock, and continue to Fiskerton Wharf and the Bromley Arms. Take care along the wharf, especially if you have children (or a wacky dog!) with you. The edge of the wharf is vertical, with a sheer drop down to the river. And no guard rail for most of the way.

❸ Turn left at the pub and left again at the road. Follow the road round a double bend, leaving the village, and take a footpath on the right. A well-defined fieldpath with excellent stiles (several of them with dog-gates) leads direct to Morton village. A dog-leg; at one point may cause confusion: ignore the side path leading off left here and resume the former line, passing to the right of a private garden to reach the road and turn left.

❹ Follow the village street past the Full Moon Inn and continue to a road junction. Turn right here, then go left, as directed by the guidepost, at a farm entrance (Fiskerton Lodge). Pass the farm and continue to the

PLACES of INTEREST

Southwell Minster — the cathedral church of the diocese of Southwell — remarkable because, contrary to popular belief, Southwell is not a city. A magnificent building, the Minster is always open to visitors. But please remember, if a service is in progress when you come, that this is a place of worship. **Reg Taylor's Swan Sanctuary**, Hill Farm Nurseries, Normanton, just north-east of Southwell, is open daily. Four lakes have been excavated to form a home for injured swans and other wildfowl. The area has developed into a nature reserve, with wildflowers. Visitors are encouraged to feed the wildfowl, and there is good access for the disabled. Telephone: 01636 813184.

end of the field. Cross the stile and turn right, then follow the hedge over the fields to the road (Gypsy Lane).

❺ Keep straight forward along Gypsy Lane, round two double bends, back to Bleasby village.

FOOD and DRINK

The Waggon and Horses on Gypsy Lane proudly boasts that it is unspoilt by progress. A cosy, traditional village inn, on a quiet side lane, with good fresh-cooked food available daily from Tuesday to Saturday, when you can choose from a wide variety of snacks, salads and main courses. And there is a special children's menu. There is no cooked food on Sundays or Mondays — but the 'doorstep' sandwiches are scrumptious! Telephone: 01636 830283. Bleasby Post Office and General Store will be able to supply the makings of a satisfactory picnic. Open daily, except Mondays. Along the way, the Hazelford Ferry Inn (telephone: 01636 830207) welcomes families and offers both restaurant facilities and bar snacks. The Bromley Arms at Fiskerton (telephone: 01636 830789) and the Full Moon Inn at Morton (telephone: 01636 830251) have both been sampled by the writer (not in the course of a single expedition!) and are also highly recommended. And — for good measure — the village post office/general store at Fiskerton will provide snack materials.

EAST BRIDGFORD

Length: 4 miles

Getting there: East Bridgford is approached via the A6097 (Fosse Way-Oxton) road; either of two junctions on the eastern side, south of Gunthorpe Bridge, leads to the village.

Public transport: Barton routes 24/24a Nottingham-Radcliffe-Gunthorpe-East Bridgford, hourly service, plus one evening run, Monday to Saturday only; Roadcar routes 53/54 Newark-Flintham-East Bridgford-Bingham, Monday to Saturday only.

Parking: There is ample space for parking alongside the main village roads.

Kneeton Road is recommended, as the route is described from there.

Maps: OS Landranger 129 Nottingham and Loughborough; Pathfinder 813 Carlton and Elston (GR 691431).

The village of East Bridgford occupies an enviable position, close to the river and with excellent lines of communication, yet securely secluded from through traffic. A pleasant, lively and compact community of some two thousand souls, there is no shortage here of worthwhile amenities and community facilities. The mining of a

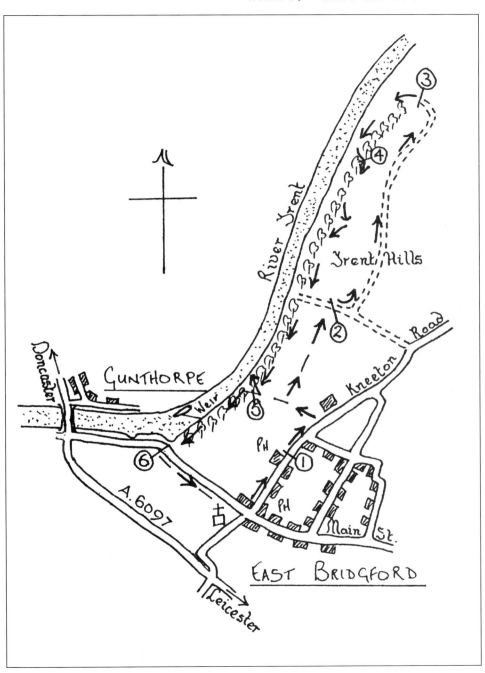

The weir at Gunthorpe.

very fine quality gypsum ceased here over 60 years ago, but agriculture remains the principal local industry, and there is a wealth of delightful walks over the Trent Hills and by the riverside.

Leaving the village on the walk, we first head off towards the river, but soon divert to follow fieldpaths and broad tracks up and over the scenic Trent Hills, where we enjoy vast and distant views across the Vale of Trent. Following a brief flirtation with the riverside meadows, we return to the hilltop, skirting around the edge of the wooded cliffside. We descend again to the riverside, to enjoy the life of the river and views of Gunthorpe, over on the far shore, with its lock, its weir and its holiday

visitors. We return to East Bridgford via a delightfully secluded fieldpath.

THE WALK

❶ Follow Kneeton Road out of the village, turning left onto a waymarked footpath just beyond the 'no limit' sign. A clear path across the centre of the field provides excellent views over the Trent valley. As the path starts to descend towards the woods, turn right onto a secondary path running parallel to the river and continue as far as a country lane.

❷ Turn right, then go left after passing through a farm gate, to follow an undulating lane over the Trent Hills, with the river coming into view, below on the left, as you proceed. Descend Old Hill, bearing left with the track to reach and cross a stile, onto the riverside fields.

❸ Follow the hedge down to a second stile and cross over, continuing round towards the river and alongside the foot of the wooded hillside. Pass a pond on your right and continue to a declivity on your left.

❹ Turn into the gap and ascend the stepped path on the right to reach the hilltop. Keep to the hedgeside path, which strays leftward for a while at one point to

PLACES of INTEREST

The village of **Gunthorpe**, just across the river from East Bridgford, is popular with visitors, particularly at summer weekends and bank holidays. There is a weir and lock here, with plenty of river life — narrow boats and cabin cruisers — and ample scope for riverside walks and picnics.

circumvent a wooded depression. Descend by steps to cross a track, then re-ascend, still keeping to the side of the hedge.

❺ Where the path meets that from East Bridgford (crossing the field from the left), turn sharp right and descend to the riverside. Turn left and follow the anglers' path, enjoying the views over the river to Gunthorpe. By the weir, note the cliff-face on your left, with its layers of gypsum and red and white clay. Continue ahead to the road.

FOOD and DRINK

The Reindeer Inn on Kneeton Road offers a full range of meals, snacks and sandwiches, from Monday to Saturday; Sunday fare is restricted to full Sunday dinners. Telephone: 01949 20227. The Royal Oak on Main Street provides drink, but not food. Telephone: 01949 20314. The wherewithal to prepare your own picnic can be obtained from the post office/general store or from East Bridgford News, both on Main Street.

❻ Cross the road and join the parallel footpath (waymarked 'Trent Valley Way'), following this delightful little path back to the outskirts of the village. Continue along the road from here back to Kneeton Road.

ASLOCKTON

Length: 5 miles

Getting there: From the direction of Nottingham, follow the A52 (Grantham) road, turning off left at the 'Whatton' sign (the old A52). Turn left again immediately before Whatton village, as directed by the guide-post, for Aslockton.

Public transport: The regular daily rail service between Nottingham and Grantham stops at Aslockton. A frequent daily bus service (Barton route 25) between Nottingham, Bingham, Grantham and Harby also calls here. Also, from Monday to Saturday, there are limited services between Newark and Bingham (Roadcar 55/56) and between Nottingham and Grantham (Reliance 625) serving Aslockton.

Parking: There should be adequate parking space available alongside Main Street. But the ideal area is outside the village, alongside the approach road from the A52 (Nottingham side).

Maps: OS Landranger 129 Nottingham and Loughborough; Pathfinder 813 Carlton and Elston and 834 Radcliffe on Trent (GR 742400).

Aslockton is noted as the birthplace of Thomas Cranmer, Archbishop of Canter-bury under Henry VIII. There is a cottage, opposite the Old Greyhound, bearing the

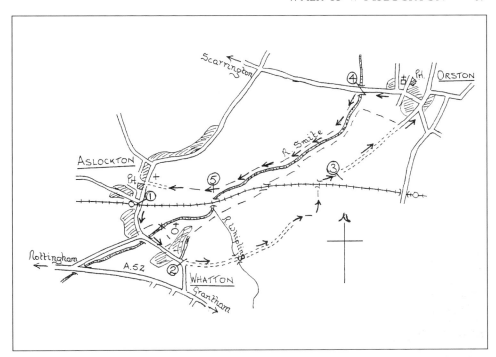

name 'Cranmer's Cottage' — though it is unlikely that this stood in the Archbishop's

time. Cranmer was, in fact, born in the manor house, which has long since disappeared, but is believed to have stood on a site behind the 19th-century church of St Thomas; this is known as Cranmer's Mound and is adjacent to an ancient motte and bailey.

This pleasant rural saunter links three of the county's quieter villages, following peaceful green lanes between Whatton and Orston and returning to Aslockton via one of our lesser-known rivers. But we start off along a splendid tree-lined avenue — following the old line of the main Grantham road.

THE WALK

❶ From Main Street, follow the road south over the railway track, turning left at

The path to Orston along Moor Lane.

the junction for Whatton, crossing the river Smite and continuing along a splendid avenue of plane trees.

❷   On the bend at the end of the avenue, leave the road, following Orston Lane, an unsurfaced track. After crossing the tiny river Whipling, this delightful rural way soon fades to a basic farm lane of twin wheel-tracks and ultimately to a perfect green lane.

After about a mile the track terminates,

crossing a drain and entering a field. Depending on the state of any growing crop, the way may not be too clear here. The correct line is approximately due east (ie, sharp right across the field) — but it may be found easier simply to follow the field boundary round to the exit point — a throughway, over a dyke, into the next field. In this field, turn left and continue, passing under the railway bridge and turning right.

❸ Keep on along the wooded path, joining Moor Lane and continuing to Orston.

Turn left in the village (signposted for Scarrington and Car Colston) and continue along Smite Lane. Ignore the first bridge (crossing the Bon Moor Drain) and continue to the next — Orston Bridge.

❹ Turn left over the stile, following the bank of the river Smite. The footpath follows the river faithfully, although there is a tendency, after passing beneath a power line, to stray to the right by continuing alongside the hedge. Ignore this, and pass through the gap between hedge and river, continuing beside the Smite for now.

❺ Just short of the railway, bear right

PLACES of INTEREST

Belvoir Castle, the Leicestershire seat of the Duke of Rutland, occupies a superb hilltop position overlooking the Vale of Belvoir, close to the village of Redmile. (The Redmile road leaves the A52 one mile east of Whatton.) The castle has magnificent staterooms, with fine pictures, tapestries and furnishings. Telephone 01476 870262 for opening hours and admission charges.

away from the river, following the right-hand side of the hedge. Continue into a second field and cross a stile on your left, following the waymark arrow to meet and join a farm track. Follow the track right, passing Cranmer's Mound, to reach the road, by the village church and Saucer Farm.

KEYWORTH

Length: 5½ miles

Getting there: Turn off the A606 (Nottingham-Melton Mowbray) road just east of Tollerton and continue through Plumtree village. The walk starts and finishes in the old village, at the southern end of Keyworth.

Public transport: Barton services 6 and 6a Nottingham-Keyworth, daily and evenings; service 12 Nottingham-Keyworth-Leicester, Monday to Saturday; also Pathfinder service S.36 Beeston-QMC-Keyworth-Cotgrave, Monday to Friday.

Parking: There is a public car park in Bunny Lane, Keyworth. You will also find a large car park — for patrons only — attached to the Salutation Inn; but ask permission if you wish to leave your wheels here during the walk.

Maps: OS Landranger 129 Nottingham and Loughborough; Pathfinder 834 Radcliffe on Trent and 854 Scalford and Nether Broughton (GR 613308).

Keyworth is one of several South Notts villages which have expanded considerably in recent years, to the extent that, today, it amounts to more of a small town. Happily, though, the old village, around the church and along Main Street and Selby Lane, has

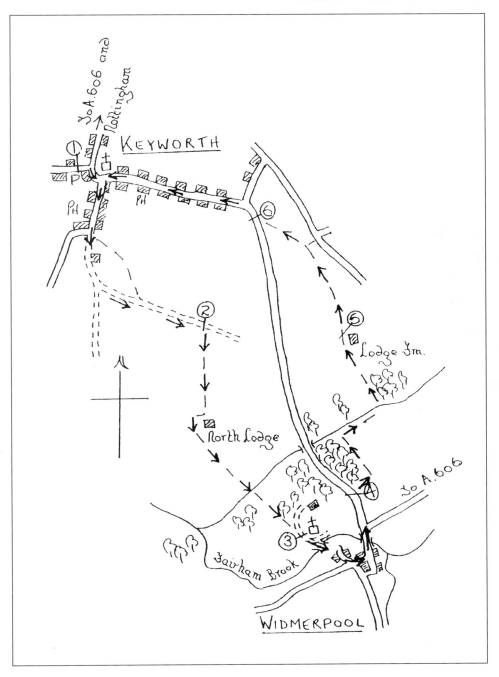

The route to Widmerpool.

managed to retain its traditional old world character. Of particular interest in the village are the church, with its splendid beacon tower, and an ancient barn on Main Street.

This walk follows quiet paths and lanes around the rolling wooded landscape of the South Notts wolds. A charming feature, around the halfway point, is the delightful, unspoilt little village of Widmerpool, with its beautiful parish church set amidst the sylvan parkland of the old hall.

THE WALK

❶   Follow Main Street south as far as the bend, continuing straight ahead here along the unsurfaced lane and passing the Lings Lane Stables. Where the track forks, take the left branch and carry on up the hill for $^1/_2$ mile.

❷   Turn right at a guidepost, following the fieldpath beside the hedge. On reaching the gateway to North Lodge Farm, turn right and follow the path round the farm boundary, as directed, along a well-kept grass track. Beyond the farm, the hedgeside is rejoined, the path continuing from here, on a clear line over fields, to the outskirts of Widmerpool. Enter the hall grounds and join the drive, where a welcome seat provides a pretty and peaceful resting place.

❸   A break in the woodland on your left, as you continue, leads through to St Peter's church; easily missed, but well worth a visit.

The chancel, with its beautiful vaulted roof, is particularly attractive. Continuing along the drive, branch right along a side path to cross Fairham Brook and reach Widmerpool — one of our county's most charming little villages, well off the beaten track and still bypassed by most modern travellers, but no doubt familiar to many generations of AA men, trained at Widmerpool Hall! Follow the road round to the left and join the Keyworth road.

Follow the road, passing the first turning on the right and continuing to a guidepost, also on your right.

❹ Cross the hedge and turn left along the side of the field, following the path around the edge of the field and two sides of the ensuing wood. Beyond the wood,

PLACES of INTEREST

Not too far north of Keyworth (about 6 miles), close to the river Trent at Adbolton Lane, Holme Pierrepont, the **National Water Sports Centre and Country Park** offers 270 acres of parkland, ideal for country walks and picnics. There are a nature reserve and fishing lagoons. The focal point of the park is the Olympic standard 2000 metre watersports course, the venue for many national and international events. Open daily; admission free (except for certain special events). Telephone: 0115 982 1212.

FOOD and DRINK

The Salutation Inn on Main Street is a roomy, traditional village pub, with a comfortable, friendly atmosphere. Families are welcome and the pub is open all day. Steaks are a speciality on a fully comprehensive menu with daily specials. Mouth-watering baguettes are also available, if you prefer a light bite. Telephone: 0115 937 2465. The Coffee Shop and Restaurant, also on Main Street, has a full and varied menu of meals, salads and snacks. Telephone: 0115 982 2895. The Plough on Selby Lane opens lunchtimes and evenings, supplying both food and drink, and families are welcome here too. Telephone: 0115 937 2479. And the village is well provided with shopping facilities.

continue into the dip, with a big modern house straight ahead. Turn right on reaching a pylon and follow the stream.

Pass a second pylon, ignoring a (private) bridge on the left, and continue to a second footbridge. Cross this one and continue, with a wood on your right, following the hedgeside to Lodge Farm.

❺ Through a little gate on the left, follow the waymarked route between the buildings and join a metalled farm road. Turn left on reaching a seat and cross a vast prairie. Continue along the fenceline over a series of paddocks and thence along a narrow enclosed footpath. From here, a further stretch of fieldpath leads to the road.

❻ Follow the road, turning left with it, and continue along Selby Lane, back to the start.

GOTHAM

Length: 6 miles

Getting there: Gotham is about 7 miles from Nottingham. Turn off the A453 (Nottingham-Ratcliffe on Soar) road at Clifton village; from here, an unclassified road leads to Gotham.

Public transport: South Notts route 1 Nottingham-Gotham-Loughborough, frequent daily service.

Parking: In The Square, Gotham (alongside the church wall).

Maps: OS Landranger 129 Nottingham and Loughborough; Pathfinder 833 Nottingham South West (GR 536301).

Gotham first achieved fame — or notoriety — in the Middle Ages, as a village of fools. Or wise men, depending on your point of view. It is said that King John intended setting up a home of some kind in the neighbourhood. The villagers, fearing the loss of their anonymity, and the imposition of a severe maintenance burden on their community, agreed that, when the royal emissaries came to spy out the land, they would try to convince them of their stupidity. The ploy succeeded, and the

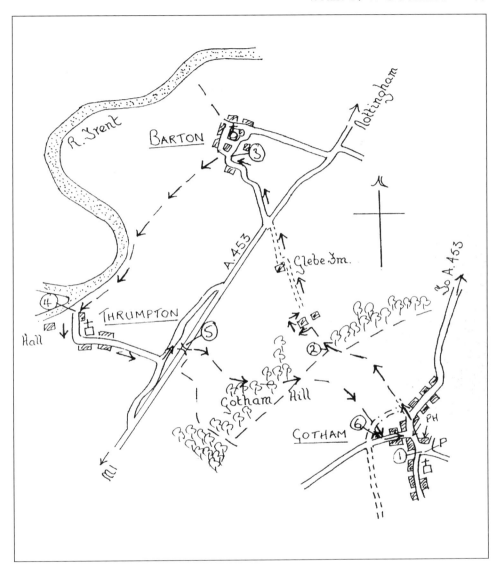

King, in his wisdom, decided to go elsewhere. Many centuries later, and despite the encroaching tentacles of modern development, the village remains a relatively quiet backwater on the unclassified road to Loughborough.

The economy of Gotham has long been tied into the mining of gypsum, used in the manufacture of plaster of Paris and plasterboard. This industry has largely died out today, and the village has become mainly a commuter community, but agriculture still

The war memorial outside the village church in Thrumpton.

flourishes in the area.

The setting of the village, with low hill-ridges to the west and north and the vast level plain of Gotham Moor to the east, offers a wide choice of excellent walks, of varying length, along well-used paths and lanes.

The route of the walk crosses the hill to the north of Gotham, descending from there to the broad Trent valley and the quiet village of Barton in Fabis. From here, a fieldpath leads to the riverside, with its wildlife, anglers and boaters. And thence to Thrumpton, a tiny one-street village with a hall — one of the traditional homes of the Byron family. After crossing, for a second time, the busy A453, the way takes us up through Gotham Hill Wood, from where we descend once more to Gotham.

THE WALK

❶ Walk north from The Square, passing the Cuckoo Bush Inn and the Kegworth Road junction. Continue along Nottingham Road as far as the bend by the British Legion Club. Keep straight forward here along the adjacent lane, past the 'Gotham Railway Walk' and on. Stay with the track, bearing left through a farm gate at its end, and follow the sunken footpath up the depression to reach the top of the hill. Follow the hedge round to the right to arrive at a stile, by the overhead wires.

❷ Cross the hilltop, enjoying the wide and distant views to Barton in Fabis and over the Trent valley. Bear left with the waymarked path, following the diverted route around the livestock buildings. Rejoin the clear farm lane and continue past Glebe Farm (the former site of a Roman villa) to the A453 road.

Cross the road, with extreme care. This is a busy link with the M1, and high speeds are all too common. Continue ahead on the quieter Barton Lane. For much of the way, the top of the floodbank provides a pleasant and welcome alternative to the actual roadway.

❸ Round the bend at 'Little Lunnon', arrive in Barton village. We are in and out of Barton in a matter of minutes, but those wishing to stay a little longer will find a tour of the village, with its medieval church and ancient ferry crossing, rewarding.

Turn left into Rectory Place, leaving by a footpath on the left, beside Old Farm. A pleasant fieldpath leads to the riverside, just outside Thrumpton village; another of those ancient river crossing points which has now lost its ferry — and its link with Long Eaton. But the anglers are still here, and the river craft and wildlife too.

FOOD and DRINK

The village of Gotham has four pubs, two of them on the route of the walk. The Sun, which is in The Square, directly opposite the car park, offers a very friendly welcome and excellent food. Telephone: 0115 983 0484. The Cuckoo Bush, nearby on Leake Road, also provides both food and drink and can be recommended. Telephone: 0115 983 0306. If you prefer a picnic, there are ample facilities for stocking up at the beginning of the walk, at the post office or Torrs Grocery on Leake Road, or the Paper Shop on Nottingham Road. There are no facilities elsewhere on the route.

PLACES of INTEREST

Although a little scarred by modern developments (housing and roads) **Clifton village**, on the A453 between Gotham and the city, retains its charm. There is a fine brick dovecote on the green and Clifton Grove, immortalised in verse by the poet Kirke White, is still a popular recreational area. South-east of Gotham, on the A60 road, the nature reserve at **Bunny Old Wood** is well worth a visit, particularly when the bluebells are in flower.

---

❹ Follow the track into Thrumpton and on along the village street, passing the entrance to Thrumpton Hall, once a home of Lord Byron. The building is not usually open to the public.

An interesting feature in the village is the 1914-18 war memorial, which takes the form of a figure of a recumbent soldier, on the outer wall of the village church. The memorial commemorates the three local men who died in the conflict.

Continue along the road and out of the village. At the junction with the old main road, turn left, then go right over the bridge to cross the A453 and turn left.

❺ Turn right at the guidepost, following the clear, straight track towards the distant woods. At the woods, bear left, climbing steeply to reach Gotham Hill. Cross the southern perimeter of the wood, keeping straight forward over the field, and descend past Gotham Primary School to Kegworth Road.

❻ Turn left back to the village.

HICKLING

Length: 4½ miles

Getting there: Turn north-east off the A606 (Nottingham-Melton Mowbray) road at Hickling Pastures, east of the A46 (Fosse Way), following Bridegate Lane for 2 miles to Hickling village. Turn left for Hickling Basin.

Public transport: Barton service 23/23a between Nottingham and Melton calls at Kinoulton and Hickling, thrice daily, Monday to Saturday. Roadcar service 29 also serves both villages, two-hourly, Monday to Saturday. There is no bus service on Sunday.

Parking: Alongside Hickling Basin (Grantham Canal) or adjacent to the village street.

Maps: OS Landranger 129 Nottingham and Loughborough; Pathfinder 834 Radcliffe on Trent and 854 Scalford and Nether Broughton (GR 691295).

Hickling, hard by the Leicestershire border, is one of Nottinghamshire's most attractive and traditional villages. Although basically a typical farming community, much of Hickling's prosperity in former years was tied to the Grantham Canal, with its basin and loading wharves, at the northern end of the village. The role of the canal has declined in the last half-century, but its attraction for anglers,

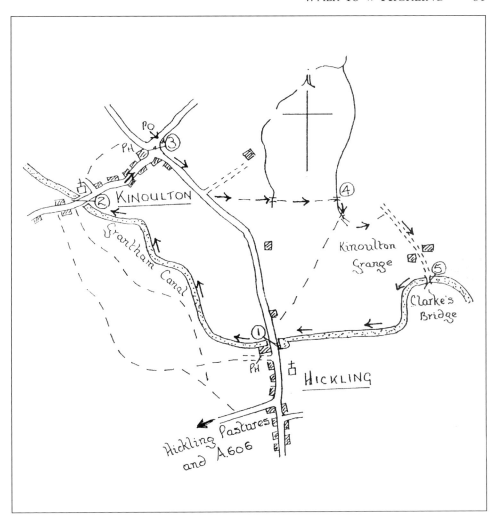

strollers and wildlife enthusiasts remains. And local children, we are told, still tremble at the tale of the giant pike which, each night at midnight, swims up the canal from Grantham to turn round in the basin, before returning to base.

This is primarily a canal walk, a stroll along the quiet waterside from Hickling to Kinoulton and back, with — just to add a little variety — a linking section through Kinoulton itself and over the fields to rejoin the canal. It is easy walking all the way, on the fringe of the glorious Vale of Belvoir.

THE WALK
❶   From the canal basin, cross the road to continue in a westerly direction, following

The Grantham Canal.

the towpath to Kinoulton. With the removal of the original bridge at Hickling, this section of the canal is no longer navigable and the channel is largely silted up in places, with consequent encroachment of reed mace adding a beauty of its own to the waterway. The journey is further enhanced by the occasional clumps, in season, of wild iris, and the presence of wildfowl: mallard, coot and waterhen.

❷   At Kinoulton, join the road and turn right. Note, in passing, the unusual brick-built parish church of St Luke. Built by Henry, Earl of Gainsborough, in the late 18th century, this building replaced the original church of St Wilfrid, which stood

¹/₂ mile away to the west of the village and had, by then, fallen into ruins.

Continue to the end of the village street, and the Nevile Arms — itself named after the Earls of Gainsborough.

❸   Turn right, following Hickling Lane. Just short of an overhead power line, pass a farm lane on your left and leave, immediately beyond here, via a waymarked footpath, also on the left. Bear right over a very large 'ridge and furrow' field. From this distance, it is not possible to identify the precise line of the path; but if you make for the extreme corner of the field, the exit — a stile in the hedgeline — will be found a little to its right.

Cross the stile and associated footbridge, and continue, now on a clear, broad, well-defined footpath. Pass beneath a power line and over a stile.

❹ If you are carrying the OS Pathfinder map, you will need to be aware that the route from here has been diverted from that shown on the map. Turn right along the hedge, as waymarked. After following this line for a little way, transfer to the right of the hedge and continue, turning left at the next bend to go on in an easterly direction, and arrive at a concrete farm road.

Turn right and follow the roadway

through, passing between the Kinoulton Grange buildings, and continuing to a stile, to the right of Clarke's Bridge. Cross the stile and descend to the canal towpath.

❺ Turn right and follow the towpath back to Hickling Basin. The channel is more open here, with more opportunity for observing wildlife. The ubiquitous coot and mallard. And perhaps a heron, or a family of swans. And an angler or two!

EAST LEAKE

Length: 5 miles

Getting there: Turn westwards off the A60 (Nottingham-Loughborough) road at the Costock bypass. East Leake is 1½ miles on from here.

Public transport: There is a good daily bus service (South Notts) between Nottingham, Gotham, East Leake and Loughborough. A less frequent service, also South Notts, runs between Nottingham, Kegworth, East Leake and Sutton Bonington — not Sundays or evenings.

Parking: There is a small free car park alongside the main village street. A few spaces are also provided opposite the parish church.

Maps: OS Landranger 129 Nottingham and Loughborough; Pathfinder 853 Loughborough North (GR 552262).

There are two 'Leakes' — East and West — both of which figure in the walk described here. East Leake is decidedly the greater of the two, having borne considerable expansion in recent years. But the heart of the village retains a genuine rural atmosphere, with a brook running alongside the village street, a small

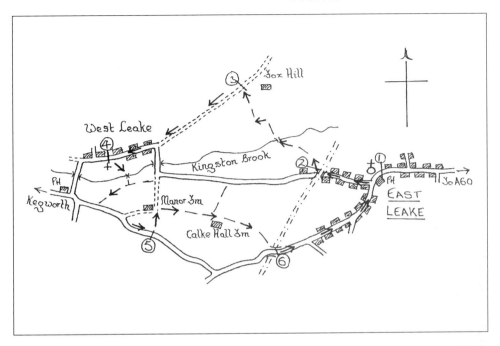

village green and an ancient pound. Local industry, over the years, has included agriculture, knitting, basket making and gypsum mining. And, we are told, shell cases were made, from locally grown willows, for use in the First World War.

Facilities include various places of worship — Anglican, Catholic, Methodist, Baptist and Evangelical — a library, health centre and fire station, junior and comprehensive schools and a leisure centre. Plus excellent shops and several pubs. And the ever-popular Rushcliffe Golf Course is nearby.

The tiny village of West Leake, a couple of miles to the west, is a complete contrast; one of Nottinghamshire's most charming rural backwaters, with ancient brick cottages, quiet lanes and a beautiful little church. In the course of a saunter along

the village street, you may meet nobody and see few vehicles. Long may it remain so.

On our walk, the West Leake road is

FOOD and DRINK

East Leake boasts three pubs, of which the Three Horseshoes (telephone: 01509 852445) is the most convenient for the walk. It is a welcoming house, with spacious and comfortable rooms, panelled walls and beamed ceilings, and you can opt for either a full meal — such as Beef and Ale Pie — or a light snack, say, a filled roll or jacket potato. Further along the road are the Nag's Head and the Bull's Head. And there is ample scope in the local shops for making up your own picnic. The Star at West Leake (telephone: 01509 852233) is a little off route, but well worth a diversion for excellent food, friendly service and traditional atmosphere.

Crossing Kingston Brook at West Leake.

followed initially, as far as the former railway station, where we join a pleasant fieldpath. After crossing Kingston Brook via an ancient brick footbridge, we climb Fox Hill, enjoying glorious distant views along the way. A left turn brings us onto the Rushcliffe to West Leake bridleway, which we follow through to West Leake itself.

We walk along the village street as far as the little church, from where we cross the fields to the south, returning to East Leake via Manor Farm and a pleasant ridge path.

THE WALK

❶ Leave East Leake via Station Road, passing beneath the railway bridge. The line (the old Great Central) has been closed for many years, but a single trackway is still in existence, with a strong possibility of future re-opening between Loughborough and Ruddington.

❷ Turn right along the former station access road, branching left immediately onto the waymarked footpath, to reach open fields. After crossing Kingston Brook via an ancient brick-built bridge, bear left to follow the hedge to a stile and continue up the wooded rise, and on around the perimeter of the fields to reach Fox Hill. It is worth pausing in the ascent to look back and enjoy the stunning views over towards Charnwood Forest.

❸ Turn left at Fox Hill, following the broad trackway through to West Leake which, unlike its eastern counterpart, is a totally unspoilt and peaceful traditional little village of red brick and pantiles, with few modern buildings. Keep straight ahead along the village street until you reach the church. Lacking either spire or tower and set back a little from the road, this could easily be missed. Look out for a footpath sign directly opposite the church gate.

❹ Turn left through the church gate and, past the church, follow a faint path between the graves and descend by steps to the neighbouring field. Cross the field diagonally left and continue, via a long footway, over the Kingston Brook. Turn right at the next gateway, crossing a big field. Through a shelter belt of trees, reach the road and turn left, passing a farm entrance, and continue to a bridleway sign (Midshires Way) on your left.

❺ Follow the hedge up to Manor Farm, turning right by the buildings and, still following the hedge on your left, along the

ridge. Pass Calke Hall Farm and continue, bearing right with the track to meet the road, close to the railway cutting.

❻ Turn left and follow Woodgate Road back to East Leake.

REMPSTONE

Length: 3¹/₂ miles

Getting there: Via the A60 (Nottingham-Loughborough) or A6006 (Hathern-Wymeswold) roads. Rempstone stands on the junction of these two roads.

Public transport: Midland Fox service 99 (Nottingham-Coalville) operates hourly, Monday to Saturday, no Sunday service. Stagecoach (United Counties) service X60 (Oxford-Nottingham) also passes Rempstone, thrice daily, Monday to Saturday, once only on Sundays.

Parking: There is ample space for parking alongside the old carriageway of Main Street (the north side of the present road).

Maps: OS Landranger 129 Nottingham and Loughborough; Pathfinder 853 Loughborough North (GR 577243).

Rempstone is a village that can easily be overlooked, despite the traffic lights on the crossroads. Indeed, for many years I was convinced that the whole community consisted of a church and a single residential property fronting onto the A60 — which was the only aspect with which I was familiar until taking the plunge and turning

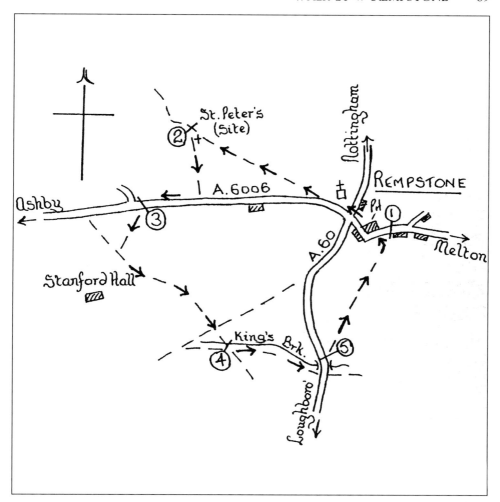

off along the Wymeswold road.

In fact, the heart of the village lies alongside this latter highway. And a most attractive little place it is too, with much traditional housing and a modicum of more recent buildings. One curious anomaly is the fact that the parish church stands aloof on the opposite side of the busy A60. Even so, the present-day (18th-century) building is much closer to the village than was its predecessor — which stood nearly a mile away in the middle of a field!

This gentle little stroll takes us along well-signposted footpaths and bridleways; first of all to the ancient site of the original parish church. Returning across the A6006 road, we follow the boundary of the Stanford Hall estate, before continuing, beside the tiny King's Brook, back to Rempstone.

The path over Sutcliffe Hill.

Although, as indicated, the paths are clearly waymarked, it is worth mentioning that most of them are not heavily used. A point in their favour.

THE WALK

❶ Cross the A60 (Loughborough) road and continue past the church. A guidepost on the right here indicates the route, leading over a vast prairie-like field to the site of the old church: St Peter in the Rushes.

There is no evidence today of the original building, much of the stonework having been used in the building of the present (1771) parish church, but the presence of a number of ancient gravestones confirms the former history of the land.

❷ Cross the graveyard area and turn left along the nearside of the hedge, following

---

FOOD and DRINK

The White Lion Inn on Main Street is a traditional, cosy little village pub, with tiled floor, low ceilings, old beams and half-timbered walls. The atmosphere is welcoming — but note the duelling pistols over the fireplace! No cooked meals are provided here, but fresh filled rolls are to be had every day, as is coffee. Telephone: 01509 880669. Rempstone has no post office or shop, so any picnic requirements will need to be brought with you.

the neglected footpath to a stile — overgrown at the time of our visit. Cross the fence and continue straight ahead over the field. On reaching the road, turn right and continue to the next junction.

❸   Turn left opposite the junction, onto a waymarked footpath and follow the right of the hedge. On reaching the Stanford Hall boundary wall, turn left onto a bridleway.

Bear left through a bridlegate and continue, still following the boundary wall and crossing Cherry Hill. Where the wall ends, continue ahead over the field to a gate and a stream — King's Brook. There is no bridge here, but there is not usually any great depth of water, and fording is easy, with the aid of a large stone in midstream. (In the unlikely event that the stream is unfordable when you come, retrace your way back over the field to an alternative footpath.)

PLACES of INTEREST

The **Great Central Railway** at Loughborough Central Station offers the experience of main line expresses, on eight miles of track, hauled by steam locos. Trains run at weekends throughout the year and daily in high season. Sunday lunch and afternoon tea can be enjoyed during the journey. For confirmation of opening times and fares, ring 01509 230726. Also in Loughborough, the **John Taylor Bell Foundry Museum** provides a fascinating and educational display, set in the world's largest bell foundry complex. Open Tuesday to Saturday and bank holidays. Telephone: 01509 233414.

---

❹   Turn left along the brook and follow through to the A60. Cross over, and turn left.

❺   Leave the road again at a guidepost on your right, following the footpath over Sutcliffe Hill, back to Rempstone village.

Tourist Information Centres covering the area include:

Mansfield: Old Town Hall, Market Place
Tel. 01623 427770
Newark: Gilstrap Centre, Castlegate
Tel. 01636 78962
Nottingham: 1-4 Smithy Row
Tel. 0115 947 0661
Ollerton: Sherwood Heath
Tel. 01623 824545
Retford: Amcott House, Grove St
Tel. 01777 860780
West Bridgford: County Hall,
Loughborough Road
Tel. 0115 977 3558
Worksop: Public Library, Memorial Avenue
Tel. 01909 501148

Bus Hotlines

Nottingham Tel. 0115 924 0000
Retford Tel. 01777 710550

Rail Enquiries

Times and fares; all national services
Tel. 0345 48 49 50